CARDIFF

A CENTENARY CELEBRATION

1905-2005

JOHN O'SULLIVAN & BRYN JONES

Sutton Publishing Limited
Phoenix Mill · Thrupp · Stroud
Gloucestershire · GL5 2BU

First published 2005

Copyright © John O'Sullivan &
          Bryn Jones, 2005

Title page photograph: The original Cardiff
Arms Hotel in the early twentieth century.

British Library Cataloguing in Publication Data
A catalogue record for this book is available from the
British Library.

ISBN 0-7509-4181-2

Typeset in 10.5/13.5 Photina.
Typesetting and origination by
Sutton Publishing Limited.
Printed and bound in England by
J.H. Haynes & Co. Ltd, Sparkford.

Cardiff Castle at the beginning of the twentieth century.

CONTENTS

A bird's-eye view of Llandaff Cathedral.

FOREWORD

by Captain Norman Lloyd Edwards

Cardiff had been the capital of Wales for thirty years and a city for eighty years when I was privileged to be Lord Mayor in 1985/86. I was a City Councillor during the exciting times when the blueprints for the future development of the city and Cardiff Bay were being debated and decided on. It was no easy task, since our forefathers had made Cardiff a city of which we can be proud, with a civic centre second to none. The developments that have taken place in the city centre, Cardiff Bay and the Millennium Stadium are in keeping with the traditions of the past. Yet it is not just bricks that made our city, but the people of many nations who live and work here. This book emphasises this and tells us of some of the great men, women and children who have contributed to Cardiff's history. I salute them and hope that future generations will be inspired by the glorious and courageous events of 1905 to 2005.

Captain Norman Lloyd Edwards
Lord Lieutenant of South Glamorgan since 1990, Lord Mayor of Cardiff 1985/86,
Prior for Wales St John Ambulance from 1989 to 2005
and former Naval ADC to The Queen.

INTRODUCTION

Incredible changes have taken place in Cardiff since the town became a city in 1905 and since it was declared capital of Wales in 1955. Many of the older houses have been demolished; the main shopping centre has been revamped; new roads have been laid and most notable of all is the development of Cardiff Bay and the construction of the Barrage. But what was Cardiff like before Christ was born? When the city status was granted in 1905, the *Cardiff Times* painted a vivid picture of the history and development of the town that had graduated to a city:

> For the beginning of Cardiff we have go back to an age when the world was two thousand years younger than in 1905. Then the Britons roamed the lowland waste which lay around the mouth of the Taff, between the mountains and the sea. The primitive dwellers hunted wild beasts among the forests. At night the howling of the wolves wakened the hills above Leckwith. Of that far-off time no authentic records remain, but the twilight dawn of the history of Cardiff merges into the light of fuller day when towards the close of the first century of the Christian era, the Roman General Aulus Didine established a military station there in the shape of a walled camp, to guard the passage of the river. It is along the line of this camp that the walls of Cardiff Castle are built.
>
> Then came the Saxons and by the time the eleventh century was reached the history of Cardiff was on a firm footing, for it was then that the Normans came. In a bloody battle just on the northern boundary of The Heath, Cardiff, the Norman battle axe o'erasme [sic] the might of the Celt, and Norman War Lord Fitzhammond divided the area of Morgannwg between them.

Cardiff remained a vibrant place throughout the ages. In the early part of the nineteenth century the postal address was Cardiff, near Llantrisant – the market town 12 miles to the north. In the 1840s and '50s thousands of refugees from the Great Irish Famine found refuge in many corners of the world, including Cardiff. The Glamorgan Canal was used to bring coal and other cargoes from the Valley towns where coal mining was established. Industrialists, especially the Bute family from the Isle of Bute in Scotland, could see great potential for Cardiff, and the small hamlet grew into a mighty port and town when the docks and railways were built. With ships from many corners of the world arriving at Cardiff, the town became home to people of many nationalities. The docks area became known as Tiger Bay, although how it got its name is something of a mystery. At the dawn of the twentieth century the port of Cardiff was one of the busiest in the world. This change in status was recognised when the former borough was made a city by Royal Charter in 1905. Fifty years later Cardiff was named as the capital of Wales, an honour long overdue.

During the next fifty years, the bulldozer had a lot to answer for, carrying on the work started by the Germans who razed Cardiff to the ground in the Second World War. Churches and chapels, without consideration for denomination, clubs and pubs, schools and shops, hotels and homes, were all reduced to piles of rubble, fit only for foundation filling for the buildings and roads planned to replace them. Not every demolished building was mourned, of course. Who can doubt the sincerity of the old lag who offered to knock down the condemned Canton Police Station without pay? The destroyers may have been hampered in their work by the solidly built fire station in Westgate Street, but they had their revenge when in less than three days they cleared, in sacrilegious haste, the 103-years-young Wood Street Congregational Chapel in an area known as Temperance Town (most of which had already been cleared in the 1930s). This is the area where the bus station was built in the postwar era.

The bulldozer showed little respect for Shakespeare, Byron or Milton, the names of the Poet's Corner streets to the east of the motor trade area of City Road. Knocked down they were, as were the homes and seamen's lodging houses in old Tiger Bay. The houses in South Dockland have also gone and so have those in Wellington Street, off Cowbridge Road East. Lower Splott suffered a slow lingering death – condemned but not destroyed with the swiftness that it warranted. 'Slums' the officials called them. Slums! – those once-proud homes in Roath and Canton, Grangetown, Newtown and Splott. Slums because they had no outside toilets and no hot water, or maybe the kitchen was a shade too small. New houses were built on what were once green fields at Rumney and Trowbridge, Llanrumney and Pentrebane, Pentwyn and Llanedeyrn, Fairwater and the Polo Field at Whitchurch. New houses for old. Modern houses with central heating, indoor toilets, fitted baths and spacious gardens, built in a clean healthy environment. New houses in exchange for the dark, dingy, damp, crumbling buildings erected in the shadow of the railways and docks, steelworks and factories that had played the major part in creating the City of Cardiff.

The Scott Memorial at Roath Park.

Cardiff – the city from which Scott of the Antarctic left on his ill-fated voyage in 1910; the city that lost thousands of men, women and children during the First and Second World Wars; the city that has produced some of the world's greatest sportsmen and women; the city that has one of the finest civic centres and university colleges in the world; the city that has a great future, with Cardiff Bay as a controversial but exciting cornerstone of what is to come; the city, finally, of which we are proud and which we love.

1905

Cardiff Made a City

There was great joy and cause for celebration when Cardiff was finally made a city on 28 October 1905, but the news failed to make banner headlines in the only local newspaper that didn't carry just advertisements on the front page – the *Cardiff Times* ran the story at the top of page four. The front page in Edwardian times was a template with the latest fashion and music notes and an article by Mabon, MP, featured every week.

News of the new status was reported to the first meeting of the City Council on Thursday 9 November 1905. The announcement was contained in a letter dated 21 October from a top civil servant, John Chalmers. It read:

> I am directed by the Secretary of State to inform you that it is His Majesty's pleasure that the Borough of Cardiff be constituted a City, and that the Chief Magistrate thereof be styled Lord Mayor. Instructions are about to be given for the issue of Letters of Patent under the Great Seal carrying His Majesty's pleasure into effect.

The monarch referred to in the letter was King Edward VII, who had never visited Cardiff. In fact, no reigning monarch had done so for 250 years. The Council's reaction to the news was to enthusiastically congratulate Alderman Robert Hughes on becoming the first Lord Mayor of the new city.

The powerful team that had lobbied for Cardiff to be made a city included the 4th Marquess of Bute, and the granting of the honour might well have been looked upon as a wedding present for him and his bride of just a few weeks. The Marquess stood alongside the Lord Mayor when he read the proclamation from the balcony. The Lord Mayor declared a public holiday for all schools in the city.

The many messages of congratulations included one from the Dean of Llandaff, who could not resist a friendly dig: 'Hearty congratulations to her new sister and Lord Mayor from the old city [of Llandaff].' The High Constable of Merthyr spoke the feelings of most in the Principality: 'Wales is proud of the distinction conferred upon its chief town.' But the reaction in Swansea carried a hint of jealousy. A former mayor of Wales' second town, an Alderman Martin, told the *Cardiff Times* that Cardiff had obtained what Swansea had not asked for. 'If Swansea was to petition for a similar honour there is no reason to believe that it would be refused,' he said. 'While the volume of trade done at Cardiff is many times greater than that of Swansea, the trade in Swansea exceeds it in value by quite as many times. Cardiff has been honoured and I trust that Swansea will be honoured too.'

In fact, it was another sixty-four years before Swansea was granted city status. The announcement was made by Prince Charles during his visit to Swansea after being invested as Prince of Wales at Caernarfon in 1969.

The elevation to city status was a costly business for Cardiff. At 1905 prices the total bill was £104, which included a fee of £7 13s 6d to the Home Office and Crown Office fees totalling £64 10s. New official stamps needed by the city cost another £30 12s. Councillors agreed that the remuneration for the position of Lord Mayor would be £1,000 a year.

The first person to be elected to the new City Council was Charles Fletcher Sanders, a building society secretary, of 14 Conway Road. He was elected for the Canton Ward in a by-election three days after Cardiff was elevated to city status. The only significant change that would have been noticed by the residents was that the name of the former Castle Road was changed to City Road. Traders and residents in City Road are set to celebrate their 100th anniversary in 2005.

What else was happening in Cardiff at the time it was made a city? Madame Adelina Patti, the acclaimed opera singer, travelled from her home in Swansea to star at a concert at the Park Hall in aid of Cardiff Infirmary. Civic dignitaries were at the Central Station to greet her and crowds lined the streets to cheer her.

Not everyone, however, was in a cheerful mood. The Shop Workers Union held a mass rally in Cathays Park to protest at the growing practice of making assistants sleep on the premises, with the shop owners stopping their board and lodgings from their pittance of a pay.

The spirit of the Religious Revival of the previous years was reflected at a meeting at the Cory Hall when the Bishop of Llandaff and leading Nonconformist ministers joined forces to urge people to sign the Temperance Pledge.

One man who could have well heeded this message was a miner from the Rhondda who, after a drinking session, stole seven herrings and six cups and saucers from Cardiff Central Station. He offered a policeman a bribe of sixpence – enough to buy two pints of beer. He was sentenced to seven days' hard labour.

On 28 June of that year, George, Prince of Wales, the future King George V, laid the foundation stone of the main university in Cathays Park. He was rewarded by being made a Freeman of the Borough, just five months before his father, Edward VII, raised Cardiff to city status.

Since Victorian times there had been a regular ferry service linking Cardiff with Penarth, but this ceased operating in 1905 and a similar facility was not reintroduced until near the end of the twentieth century, after the building of Cardiff Barrage.

The odds are that if people in a pub quiz were to be asked why 1905 is noteworthy they would be unlikely to say it was the year Cardiff was made a city. For in a country where rugby is a religion, 1905 was the year that Wales beat the New Zealand All Blacks by one try (three points in those days) to nil. It was the first All

Blacks tour to the United Kingdom and Ireland, and they won every one of their other twenty-seven matches. Wales, unbeaten at home for six years, thrilled the crowd at the Cardiff Arms Park when Ted Morgan scored the historic try. Before the kick-off Morgan led the 47,000 spectators in singing the Welsh National Anthem. There is one memorial to the match – the Gwyn Nicholls Gates on the Westgate side of the Millennium Stadium. Gwyn, who was known as the 'prince of Welsh centres', was captain of the 1905 side that beat the All Blacks. He was the first Welshman to play for a British XV when he toured Australia in 1899, won twenty-four Welsh caps, and skippered Wales ten times, as well as being captain of the Cardiff team.

Gwyn Nicholls.

1906

City Hall Opens

Cardiff's Civic Centre is considered one of the finest in the world. The crowning glory is the City Hall, which was officially opened, together with the neighbouring Law Courts, by the 4th Marquess of Bute on 29 October 1906. Architects Lanchester, Stewart and Rickards won the contract to design the £129,000 building – less than the cost of an average house in Cardiff a hundred years later. The Law Courts cost £96,000. Another £190,000 was spent in purchasing and laying out Cathays Park. E. Turner and Sons started the construction work in 1900, and the buildings were almost complete by the time Cardiff was made a city in 1905. The statues on the top of the 194ft clock tower represent the four winds. They were sculpted by Henry Charles Fehr, a giant in his art in late Victorian and Edwardian days. He also sculpted the Welsh Dragon on top of the City Hall.

Portland stone was used in the construction of the most prominent buildings in the Civic Centre. A total of eleven million bricks were used in the building of the City Hall and Law Courts. If extended end to end, the bricks would have stretched for 500 miles. The weight of the stone used was 15,700 tons; some 54 tons of lead were also used in the buildings; and the marble columns weighed a total of 87 tons. There was a total of 25 miles of heating and hot water pipes and 100 miles of electrical wiring. The National Museum of Wales was opened by King George V on 21 April 1927, four days before Cardiff City won the FA Cup.

'If music be the food of love, play on. . .' These were the first words spoken by an actor on the stage of Cardiff's New Theatre when it opened on 10 December 1906. The play was William Shakespeare's *Twelfth Night*; the actor was Beerbohm Tree, who played the part of Duke Orsino. The opening words were most appropriate for the launch of the New Theatre where much music has been played in its history.

Greek seamen began to settle in Cardiff in 1872, and by 1906 the community was strong enough to open a Greek Orthodox church – a fine domed building that is a landmark in Bute Street. The first Greek priest was Fr John Georgiades. The constitution for Cardiff was approved by the King of Greece in 1910. A Greek school and community centre were added in 1915.

One of the many statues in Cardiff is that of John Cory, later Baron Cory, in Cathays Park. His name is also remembered in the Coryton area of Whitchurch. The statue was unveiled on 21 June 1906, a decade after the Cory Memorial Temperance Hall

Evan Roberts

was donated to Cardiff in memory of John's father, Richard Cory. The unveiling of Cory's statue happily coincided with the Great Revival, during which the famous West Wales preacher Evan Roberts got thousands of people throughout the world to sign the Temperance Pledge. It is believed that he held at least one of his meetings at the Cory Hall.

Cardiff remained a champion in the fight against evil drink with Temperance Town being built around the Temperance Hall (later Wood Street Congregational Chapel). The maze of narrow streets that made up Temperance Town were demolished in the 1930s, and after the Second World War the site became Central Square and the main bus station. As Cardiff celebrated its 100th anniversary, the temperance tradition had disappeared. Pubs and clubs were flourishing, and there was concern about binge drinking among young people. One wonders what John Cory, who died on 27 January 1910, would have thought of this.

The Royal Hamadryad Seamen's Hospital opened in the docks area in 1906, replacing a ship of the same name that had been used as a hospital throughout the Victorian and early Edwardian days.

1907

Historic Royal Visit

When the Royal Yacht sailed into the port on Friday 12 July 1907, it signalled the start of the first visit to Cardiff by a reigning monarch for 250 years. Aboard the vessel was King Edward VII and Queen Alexandra, who had come to open the dock which had been named after her. The dock had been carved out of the foreshore at a cost of £1.5 million by the Cardiff Railway Company, headed by the 4th Marquess of Bute. The official opening was performed by the Royal Yacht cutting a ribbon between the lock and the dock. The King and Queen and their daughter Victoria were cheered by thousands of people as the historic event took place.

The *Cardiff Times* reported that their Majesties had stood on the bridge of the yacht and looked round at the blurred picture of masts, funnels, streamers, flags and human heads. When the royal family left the yacht, the King removed his sword from its scabbard and knighted the Lord Mayor, William Smith Crossman, as he knelt on the quayside. The setting was perfect for such a ceremony, for the Lord Mayor had come to Cardiff from the West Country in 1884 to work on the

Crowds gathered in Queen Street to greet King Edward VII and Queen Alexandra.

Horse-drawn baker's van in Ely, 1907.

construction of Roath Dock. He was an ardent trade unionist and one of the leaders of the major building trade dispute in Cardiff in 1892. At the end of the dispute, a Labour Progressive League was formed in Cardiff and Crossman was elected as a Liberal–Labour candidate, representing the Cathays Ward on the old Town Council. He was the first Labour Lord Mayor of Cardiff.

The royal event crowned a great year for the city. On New Year's Day Cardiff Rugby Club beat the touring South Africans 17–0 at the Cardiff Arms Park.

She was a handsome woman, with large expressive eyes and a wealth of curly golden hair, who had had a first-class education at a private boarding school on the outskirts of London. She was Leslie James, the only woman to be hanged for murder at Cardiff Prison. She was hanged by the two Pierrepoint brothers at 8 a.m. on Wednesday 14 August 1907. Successive Home Secretaries had reprieved every South Wales person sentenced to death since 1876, but no mercy was shown to 40-year-old James, a mother of two, who had been found guilty of murdering a day-old baby from Fleur-de-Lis who had been placed with her for adoption. The infant had died on a train. James was labelled as a baby farmer, someone who accepted unwanted babies to place for adoption.

In the 1960s a dismantled aeroplane was discovered in the garage of a house in Blackweir, Cardiff. It was a monoplane, made by local aviation pioneer Charles Watkins, who said that in 1907 it was the first plane to fly over Cardiff at night. Charles agreed to donate it to the museum at RAF St Athan. Some experts claimed that it could never have flown; others were more inclined to believe Watkins, who was closely questioned

The monoplane built by Charles Watkins.

whenever he visited St Athan. The monoplane, called the Robin Goch, was transferred to the National Museum of Wales in Cardiff but is to go on permanent display at the Maritime Museum in Swansea. Charles Watkins died in Cardiff in the 1970s.

1908

Lloyd George Honoured

A great Welshman, David Lloyd George was made a Freeman of Cardiff in 1908. A Welshman? He was born in Manchester, true, but he had enough Welsh blood in his veins to play for Wales, he prayed and preached like a Welshman, and he was fluent in the language. He can be counted as Welsh for no other reason than his oratory matched that of anyone else from Wales. If anyone still has doubts about his Welshness they should be reminded of his speech when he was made a Freeman. He referred to Cardiff as the greatest city of the land he loved best.

The First World War was two years old when the Liberal Lloyd George, who was Minister for Munitions, collaborated with the Conservatives to succeed Herbert Asquith as Prime Minister. He held the post until 1922, when he was forced out by Conservative members of the cabinet. He spent the rest of his political life as a backbencher. David Lloyd George died at the age of 84 on 26 March 1945.

David Lloyd George in Cardiff.

Three contemporary Welsh boxers and all British Champions. Left to right: Freddie Welsh (lightweight), Tom Thomas (middleweight) and Jim Driscoll (featherweight).

Paolo Radmilovic earned himself a place in the Hall of Fame by competing in five Olympic Games (six if you count the unofficial games in Athens in 1904). He won no fewer than four gold medals, all of them as a member of the British polo team. He was the first British sportsman to have a plaque in the American Hall of Fame.

Two other sporting landmarks were achieved in 1908. Riverside Football Club became Cardiff City AFC, and Jim Driscoll, who was then not known as 'Peerless Jim', won the Empire featherweight title in London when he beat Charles Griffin on points over fifteen rounds on 24 February. The fight was also billed as the British version of the World Featherweight title.

Whitchurch Hospital opened and was given the unfortunate title of 'lunatic asylum', which nowadays is no longer used. Whitchurch was used as a military hospital in both world wars and did tremendous work, especially for shell-shock victims. The hospital also has one of the finest units in the country for dealing with alcoholics and drug addicts as well as caring for people with depression.

A horse-drawn bus in Whitchurch, 1908.

1909

Magnetic South Pole Discovered

Scott of the Antarctic was not the only great explorer to have links with Cardiff (*see* 1910). In 1909 a man who was born in St Fagans was one of three men who were the first to reach the magnetic South Pole. He was Professor Edgeworth David, who with his companions, Sir Douglas Mawson and Alistair Mackay, was part of Ernest Shackleton's British Antarctic Expedition from 1907 to 1909. When they reached the South Pole, they claimed the surrounding land for the British Crown, and named it Victoria Land.

At that time the magnetic pole lay within the Antarctic continent at latitude 71.6°S and longitude 152°E. In the twenty-first century it is lying far out to sea at latitude 65°S and longitude 139°E. and is travelling 10 to 15 kilometres north-westerly each year. Electric currents and the rolling motion of the liquid iron core of the Earth dictate the position of the magnetic poles.

Tannatt Edgeworth David was born at St Fagans in 1858 to the Revd William David and his wife, Margaret (née Thompson). Edgeworth, the name by which he was best known, emigrated to Australia in 1882, when he was 24 years of age where he was appointed as assistant geological surveyor for the New South Wales government. He married Carolina Mallet, a fellow passenger on the voyage to Sydney. In 1897 Edgeworth and his wife joined an expedition to investigate the origin of a coral reef formation in the Pacific Ocean.

Professor Edgeworth David, who discovered the South Magnetic Pole in 1909. *(Anne Edgeworth Smith)*

Edgeworth was Professor of Geology and Physical Geography at the University of Sydney from 1891 to 1924. He was knighted in 1920 and was honoured with a Commonwealth and State funeral when he died at the age of 76 in 1934.

Godfrey Morgan, the first Viscount Tredegar, was one of the 600 members of the Light Brigade who rode into the 'Valley of Death' during the Crimean War in 1854. It was therefore fitting that both he and his horse, Sir Briggs, were honoured when a statue of Tredegar astride Sir Briggs was unveiled in Cardiff in October 1909 on the day the Viscount was made a Freeman of the City.

There was great excitement in Cardiff on 20 August 1909 when the first passengers and mail to arrive in Wales on the *Mauritania* came by train from Fishguard, where the liner had docked. The liner, which was to hold the Blue Riband for the fastest Atlantic crossing for thirty years, was used as a troop ship during the First World War before returning to commercial service. It was scrapped in 1935.

❖   ❖   ❖

The maiden flight of Cardiff-born Ernest Willows' first airship took place on 26 November 1909, a month after the University College main building opened in the city. It was also the year that the first permanent Cinema Electra opened in the city and the year that James Howells, founder of Cardiff's most famous store, died.

1910

Scott of the Antarctic

Events which brought great joy and then great sadness linked Cardiff with one of the biggest news stories in its hundred years' history. The joy came in June 1910 when Cardiff played host to Captain Robert Falcon Scott and the crew of the *Terra Nova*, which had come to the port to take on coal for its historic and tragic journey to the Antarctic. The sorrow came when Scott and five of his men died after reaching the South Pole.

Scott and his officers were guests at a banquet in their honour at the Royal Hotel. The Lord Mayor proposed a toast to the *Terra Nova* and its crew, whose journey to the South Pole would be the biggest expedition ever to leave Cardiff. In response, Scott acknowledged the tact and zeal of his second in command, Lt Evans, in canvassing South Wales for subscriptions for the expedition. The industrialists had responded with donations of more than £5,000 and free coal for the *Terra Nova* bunkers.

When the banquet was over the crew of the *Terra Nova* joined the main guests for a smoking concert, during which the Lord Mayor presented Scott with a banner emblazoned with the arms of the city. The next day the *Terra Nova* left Cardiff with the banner flying from its masthead together with a giant leek, an emblem of Wales.

Scott wrote to the Lord Mayor thanking him and the citizens of Cardiff and South Wales for the magnificent send-off that the expedition had received. He added: 'We feel that such an expression of warm sympathy and hearty goodwill is an inspiration of success.' This was not to be. Scott reached the South Pole on 18 January 1912, only to find that the Norwegian Captain Roald Amundsen had got there first. Disaster struck as Scott's party struggled through blizzards in an attempt to reach the *Terra Nova*. Petty Officer Edgar Evans, from Swansea, was the first to die, of natural causes. The bodies of Scott and four others were found by a search team on 10 November 1912.

The world was rocked by the news, but nowhere was the loss felt more than in Cardiff, the city which had wished a *bon voyage* to the *Terra Nova* some twenty-nine months earlier. Those who attended the banquet then filled the pews of St John's Church for a memorial service, during which special prayers were offered for the dead men – Robert Falcon Scott, Lawrence Edward Grace Oates, Edward Adrian Wilson, Henry Robertson Bowers and Petty Officer Edgar Evans from Swansea. Hundreds of people gathered around the church and joined in the hymns to music played by military bands.

All the papers and diaries of the victims were recovered, but the search party decided to leave the bodies in the frozen ice where they died. (For the return of the *Terra Nova, see* 1913.)

One of the most amazing funerals in Cardiff was that of John White, the father of the successful amusement caterer Sidney White. Before he died of a heart attack at the age of 76 in 1910, John asked his son to take his body to the cemetery on one of the fairground traction engines. The giant machine was draped in purple and black and bedecked with many floral tributes.

Alexandra Gardens, in Cathays Park, and the Globe Cinema, in Albany Road, both opened in 1910, adding to the growing leisure facilities in the city.

The funeral of showman John White.

1911

Seamen's Strike

Winston Churchill was condemned for sending soldiers to Tonypandy in an attempt to break the 1910 strike by miners, but this did not deter the then Home Secretary from sending troops to Cardiff during the seamen's strike of 1911. Churchill had 25,000 troops standing by in London and sent battalions to ports throughout Britain because he feared the strike would interfere with food cargoes.

Cardiff Docks were brought to a complete standstill as seamen, fighting for better wages and conditions at sea and on shore, answered the call of the National Sailors' and Firemen's Union. Railwaymen went on strike at the same time and the tension was such that, after the Riot Act had been read at Llanelli, the troops opened fire and killed two strikers.

❖   ❖   ❖

Pioneer aviator Benjamin Charles Hucks was the first pilot to fly an aircraft across the Bristol Channel. He made the historic flight from Weston-super-Mare to Cardiff on 1 September 1911.

A strike by seamen brought Cardiff to a halt; Hancock Wilson and Cllr Chapell (left) were among those who negoiated a settlement.

The Central Cinema, which opened in The Hayes, Cardiff, on 7 March 1911, was the scene of a major incident during the First World War. Boxer 'Peerless' Jim Driscoll went there while on leave from the Army and made a citizen's arrest of a German-born photographer whom he accused of being a German spy. The man had angered the boxer by refusing to stand for the national anthem.

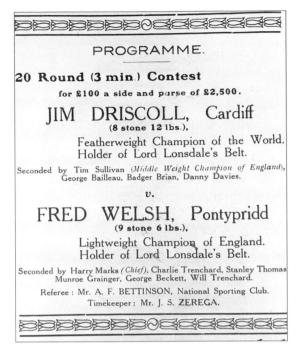

The programme for the match between 'Peerless' Jim Driscoll and Fred Welsh.

1912

Victims of the Titanic

Boxing fans in Cardiff and the Valleys wept unashamedly when they learnt that two young Welsh boxers were among the 1,500 people who died when the liner *Titanic* sank after hitting an iceberg on her maiden voyage. The story of how Leslie Williams and Dai Bowen came to be aboard the ill-fated liner was told by South Wales boxing referee Charles Barnett. He had been asked by Pittsburgh millionaire Frank Torreyson to send out two Welsh boxers whom he would sponsor in America. Barnett's first choice was the great Jimmy Wilde, the future world flyweight champion, who died in Cardiff in 1969; second choice was Newport lightweight Johnny Basham.

Leslie Williams and Dai Bowen: two unfortunate pugilists who drowned in the *Titanic* disaster.

Both men turned down the offer, but Williams and Bowen jumped at the chance. They were to be paid £5 a week pocket money, given free board and lodging and travelling expenses as well as all they earned in the boxing ring. Originally booked to sail on the liner *Baltic*, they switched to the *Titanic* to give themselves time to have new suits made for the trip. They were delighted that there was a gym on board the *Titanic* as they could train during the voyage. However, they travelled third class and had no hope of survival when the liner sank on 15 April 1912.

Both boxers are believed to have fought in Cardiff for shillings in the boxing booth run by Jack Scarrott. Williams left a widow and a son, who became a teacher after being helped through college by a fund set up in memory of the boxers.

King George V visited Cardiff on 26 June to lay the foundation stone for the National Museum of Wales. The Coal Exchange reopened on 20 February after refurbishment and the Old Glamorgan County Hall in Cathays Park also opened this year.

The arrival of Billy the Seal at Victoria Park Zoo caused excitement. Billy was the main attraction at the zoo until she died in 1939 (see p. 59). It was only after her death that it was realised Billy was, in fact, a female. Her remains are held at the National Museum of Wales. A statue in her honour was unveiled at Victoria Park by the folk singer Frank Hennessy, who also immortalised Billy in song.

1913

The Terra Nova Returns

Almost three years to the day after the *Terra Nova* had been given a great send-off from Cardiff, the vessel that had carried Captain Robert Scott and his crew on their ill-fated voyage to the Antactic returned to the city where Scott and the other four men who died were still being mourned. The *Terra Nova* was lying off Flat Holm, with the banner carrying the Cardiff Coat of Arms flying at her foremast – the banner had been presented to Scott at a farewell banquet at the Royal Hotel, St Mary Street, in June 1910. The Red Dragon was flying from the *Terra Nova*'s main mast.

Among those aboard the *Terra Nova* as she entered Cardiff Docks was Captain Scott's widow and her young son, Peter, who was carried along the deck by a burly sailor. The cheering was led by a gang of boys swimming near the mudflats, opposite the Channel Dry Docks. Hundreds of

The figurehead of the *Terra Nova*.

schoolchildren waiting at the docks joined in the welcome for the survivors of the expedition and for Lady Scott and Peter. The greatest cheer came when Commander Evans held young Peter on the side of the vessel and the boy, wearing the Commander's white peaked hat, saluted the crowd. The crowd fell silent as the *Terra Nova* pulled alongside the south-west corner of the East Basin from where she had left, carrying the hopes of a nation, three years earlier.

The roots of the National Association of Schoolmasters can be traced to Cardiff in 1913. George Cording, who worked in the city, was the first man to realise that the National Union of Teachers (NUT) was not working in the best interests of the men in the profession. He formed his own association in Cardiff to oppose the NUT's campaign for equal pay for women teachers. By 1922 the National Association of Schoolmasters was strong enough to make a complete break from the NUT.

There was an unusual road accident in Penarth Road, Cardiff, in April 1913. A drayman from Hancock's Brewery was killed when his team of horses bolted near the old toll-gate when he was returning from Barry to Cardiff. Twenty-eight-year-old Ivor Marsh, from Holmsedale Street, Grangetown, clung to his dray for a hundred yards and died when it collided with a van.

This was the year that the Mansion House on the corner of Richmond Road became the official residence of the Lord Mayor and also when the Rhiwbina Garden Village was established.

1914

The First World War Starts

Britain declared war on Germany on 4 August 1914, but for Cardiff the war had started twenty-four hours earlier when sailors from all over South Wales answered calls to report to naval bases, including those in Plymouth and elsewhere in Devon. Sixty men were called up from Cardiff, and the General Station was packed with relatives and friends who had come to see them off. There were so many people there that the gates had to be closed. By midnight there were 300 men boarding trains, leaving behind them weeping women and children. The *South Wales Echo* reported that the sailors and the crowds bidding them farewell sang patriotic songs with great gusto. The Salvation Army band from Grangetown escorted one of their members, a naval reservist, to the station. He had received his call-up papers while leading a

Sunday school class. The band stayed at the station and played hymns, which were sung with great enthusiasm. Cheers rang out as the special troop trains steamed out of Cardiff taking the men to war.

Sadly it was a sailor, Stoker First Class William Welton, who was the first Cardiff man to die in action. He was serving on HMS *Amphion*, which was sunk with the loss of all hands, after hitting a mine in the North Sea on 6 August 1914, when the war was only two days old. An old boy of St Patrick's School, Grangetown, he was just 21 when he was killed, along with 130 shipmates aboard the *Amphion*, which had been built at Pembroke and launched there a year earlier.

The army did not start major recruiting until the second week of September 1914. The main recruiting depot was at Gladstone Road School, not far from Maindy Barracks in Cathays. Up to a hundred men a day queued to join the Cardiff Pals, the proud title given to the men who joined the Colours at Gladstone Road School or at the Cardiff Horse headquarters in Park Place. Orders were given that the men were to be drilled without arms but would not be paid until they were considered fit to be in the army. The 4th Marquess of Bute allowed Blackweir Farm to be used for training purposes, and tents and field kitchens were erected there. Among those in charge of the training was Sergeant Charles Burley Ward of The King's Own Yorkshire Light Infantry. He moved to Cardiff after earning the Victoria Cross in South Africa in 1900.

South Wales miners did more than their bit for the cause. They voted to work an extra hour a day and on Sundays to keep British ships supplied with coal.

Germans living in Cardiff and sailors aboard German ships in the docks found themselves stranded. The United States did not join the fight against Germany until 1917 so the American Consul in Cardiff agreed to look after the interests of Germans in South Wales, many of whom were destitute and homeless. The National Sailors' and Firemen's Union made sure that the German Merchant Navy men did not starve. They hoped that Germany would be equally generous to British sailors stranded in their country.

As recruits from all parts of South Wales flocked to Cardiff the *South Wales Echo* published on a Sunday for the first time. Banner headlines, which replaced advertisements on the front page, told of massive German setbacks, with 30,000 prisoners being taken in Belgium. This belief led to the saying 'It will all be over by Christmas.' Sadly four Christmases were to pass before peace came on 11 November 1918 – at the eleventh hour of the eleventh day of the eleventh month.

It was not just the war that made news in 1914. The old Town Hall in St Mary Street was demolished and the Bishop's Palace at Llandaff was destroyed by fire. It was also the year that the Principality Buildings opened in Kingsway and when Llandaff Cinema, later renamed The Tivoli, showed its first films. And a star was born! Singer and comedienne Tessie O'Shea made her world debut on 31 March.

1915

MP Killed by Sniper

Thousands of Welshmen died in action during the First World War, but it was a Scotsman killed by a sniper's bullet in France on 2 October 1915 who was mourned as much as anyone in Cardiff. He was Lord Ninian Crichton-Stuart, who was Conservative MP for the city, and died at the age of 32 while commanding the 6th Battalion of the Welsh Regiment during the Battle of Loos. Lord Ninian, who was born in 1883, was the son of the 3rd Marquess of Bute and his wife Gwendoline. After entering politics in Scotland, Lord Ninian was elected as an MP for Cardiff in 1910 and still held the seat when he led his battalion into action. He is buried in Béthune Military Cemetery in France. A requiem mass for him was celebrated at St David's Cathedral, Cardiff, and memorial services were held in churches and chapels throughout the city. A statue can be seen near the National Museum and Galleries in Cathays Park, and for decades the Lord Ninian Hospital, in Cathedral Road, carried his name.

Fifteen Welshmen were awarded the Victoria Cross during the First World War. Cardiff-born Frederick Barter was 24 when he was awarded the Victoria Cross, the highest and most prestigious award for gallantry in the face of the enemy

The Lord Ninian Hospital, Cathedral Road, was named in memory of the Cardiff MP who was killed during the First World War.

The flags were out in Daniel Street, Cathays, for Sergeant Fred Barter (below). He was the only Cardiff man to win the Victoria Cross during the First World War.

that can be presented to British and Commonwealth forces. Barter was serving with the 1st Battalion of the Royal Welch Fusiliers at Festubert, France, on 16 May 1915. He called for volunteers and, with the eight men who responded, he attacked the enemy position with bombs, capturing three German officers, 102 men and 500 yards of their trenches. He subsequently found and cut eleven of the enemy's mine leads situated about twenty yards apart. He later achieved the rank of Captain and was also awarded the Military Cross. He died at the age of 60 at Poole, on 15 May 1953, the day before the thirty-eighth anniversary of his heroic deed. His VC is displayed at the Royal Welch Fusiliers Museum at Caernarfon Castle.

1916

The Killing Fields

Nearly 35,000 Welshmen, including many from Cardiff, were killed in action during the First World War. Most of the Welshmen died in Belgium and France and up to the border with Switzerland. Others died in Greece. War graves can be found at Ypres, Passchendaele, Mons, the Somme and Verdun.

Some of the fiercest battles were fought in Mametz Wood, where 4,000 Welshmen were killed in three days during July 1916. Mametz Wood was lost, but Welsh troops recaptured it in the summer of 1918 in a battle that prompted one war correspondent to liken their action to Cardiff City playing at their best. It was reported that one out of ten men from one German battalion were shot for refusing to go to the front line.

In 1987 a metal sculpture of a Red Dragon, by David Peterson, was erected at Mametz Wood to commemorate the sacrifice of the 38th (Welsh) Division. There are signs in the Welsh language and money for the memorial was raised by public subscription. The Welsh Regiment provided a total of thirty-five battalions during the war winning a total of seventy-one battle honours though at a cost of 8,360 casualties.

Jim Flynn, of Grangetown, Cardiff, learning to fire a machine gun in the First World War. He was later wounded and was carried three miles to a field hospital by a German soldier. His children include Paul Flynn MP and former Cardiff Councillor Mike Flynn. (*Mike Flynn*)

The Victoria Cross was awarded to Hubert William Lewis, for his heroism when fighting with the Cardiff Pals at Macukovo, Greece in 1916. Although severely wounded he rescued an injured comrade and carried him to safety. Lewis, from Milford Haven, was one of many volunteers from various parts of Wales who travelled to Cardiff to join the Pals in 1914.

The battleship HMS *Colossus* was commanded by Admiral Jellicoe during the Battle of Jutland in 1916, and no doubt he was in the audience when the ship's band, The Ten Loonies, entertained the 750 men on board. Five sailors from Cardiff were members of the band. They were known as Snuffy Atkinson, Birdie Green, Steamboat Phillips, Whacker Morgan and Digger Long.

David Lloyd George was Secretary of State for War when he came to Cardiff to unveil the statues in the Marble Hall at the City Hall. The statues, a gift from Lord Rhondda, mainly depict the heroes of Wales, including Alfred Turner's *Owain Glyn Dŵr* (1354–1416); Ernest Gillick's *Harri Tewdwr* (Henry VII; 1457–1509); Goscombe John's *St David*, the Patron Saint of Wales; and Havard Thomas's *Boadicea*, widow of King Pratagus, of the Celtic Iceni tribe who died in AD 61.

1917

The Heat of the Battle

The 16th (Service) Battalion, formed at Cardiff in November 1914 by the Lord Mayor and City Council, saw action in France. In April 1917, a battalion of the South Wales Borderers entered Baghdad and the following December two battalions of the Welch Regiment were given a great reception when they entered the City of Jerusalem with General Allenby's force. The 3rd Reserve Battalion, raised in Cardiff in August 1914, remained in the city throughout the war. Cyclist battalions, which were formed in Cardiff, were based in Britain for the duration.

Among those who died at Pilkem Ridge in Belgium was the North Wales sheep farmer Ellis Humphrey Evans, who was one of the most notable bardic poets of all time. Writing under the name of Hedd Wyn ('White Peace') he was posthumously awarded the Bardic Chair at the National Eisteddfod at Birkenhead in September 1917, for a poem he wrote while serving in the battlefield. The chair was draped in black after he had been declared the winner, a month after he had been killed in action.

Captain Richard Wain was just 20 years old, and serving in the Tank Corps when he became one of the youngest posthumous holders of the Victoria Cross. The officer from Llandaff, Cardiff, was serving at Marcoing, near Cambrai, France on 20 November 1917 and was one of only two survivors when his tank was disabled by a direct hit near an enemy strong point which was holding up the British advance. The *London Gazette* reported on 13 February 1918 that, although bleeding profusely, Captain Wain refused the attention of the stretcher-bearers, rushed from behind the tank with a Lewis gun and captured the strong point, taking about half the garrison prisoners. Despite his severe wounds, he then picked up a rifle and continued to fire at the enemy until he received a fatal wound to the head.

Back home in Cardiff, older schoolchildren were given the task by the War Office of making sandbags to protect buildings from German bombs, and women taxi drivers were allowed for the first time. Women had been driving trams since 1915.

Meanwhile the development of Cardiff continued and a new fire station with a tall observation tower was built in Westgate Street. The tower became a popular nest for hundreds of seagulls who noisily objected when the building was demolished in the 1960s.

1918

First World War Ends

On 11 November 1918, the *Western Mail* siren signalled the signing of the Armistice, at the request of the Germans. All were wildly excited. Schoolchildren ceased work and listened to the bells and hooters. They cheered and sang songs and were dismissed for the day after prayers of thanksgiving. The *Cardiff Times* report of the peace celebrations are worth recording:

> St Mary Street, Queen Street and other leading thoroughfares were filled with excited crowds. Processions sprang up as if by magic at every street corner, and in less time than it takes to tell, the whole city was en fête. Flags and streamers flew from every building and the bells of St John's Church rang out a merry peal. One limbless soldier was wheeled down St Mary Street, ringing a bell with the vigour of a muffin man. Others waved flags, some sang the National Anthem, a few blew on combs and others shouted through extemporised megaphones, but they were all different ways of expressing the same thing – uncontrollable delight that the long nightmare had passed and that the dawn of peace had come. Tramway drivers and conductresses joined in the celebrations and all services came to a halt. Work stopped at the docks and all the shops closed.
>
> Tramway girls, who had been recruited during the war, were cheered as they joined wounded soldiers in procession. The crowds sang to music provided by the Salvation Army Band and the Cardiff Naval Brigade band. Children added to the noise by banging on bully beef tins and other items.

University students in caps and gowns paraded the streets, stopping here and there to give the College war cry. French sailors were cheered but the greatest heroes of the day were the men who wore the Mons Ribbon. It showed that the public realised their debt of gratitude to the Old Contemptibles. In St Mary Street a life-size effigy of the German leader, the Kaiser, was suspended by the neck on a rough-and-ready gallows. By contrast, thanksgiving services were held in churches and chapels of all denominations. The Lord Mayor described it as the greatest day in the history of the world.

Just nineteen months after being launched by the wife of the Prime Minister, David Lloyd George, the cruiser HMS *Cardiff* earned a unique place in history. As the flagship of the Sixth Light Cruiser Squadron the *Cardiff* led the seventy-four ships of the defeated German Navy into Scapa Flow in Scotland on 21 November 1918. The German ships, still manned by their own crews, who were virtually prisoners, became a tourist attraction at Scapa Flow.

Rear Admiral von Reuter, the German Officer in command at Scapa Flow, knew that Germany would have to accept surrender terms so when the *Cardiff* and the best part of the British Fleet left for exercises he gave the order for the German fleet to be

HMS *Cardiff* hit the headlines when it led the defeated German fleet into Scapa Flow.

The Great Naval Surrender.

German Armada Led In by H.M.S. Cardiff.

THE EX-KAISER.

Sept. 6th, 1890.—My navy will be able to accomplish any task which I may have to give it.

Oct. 23rd, 1898.—Our future lies on the waters.

1904 (to the Czar).—From the Admiral of the Atlantic to the Admiral of the Pacific.

ADMIRAL BEATTY.

[SIGNAL MADE NOV. 21st., 1918.]

The German flag is to be hauled down at 3.57 to-day, and is not to be hoisted again without permission.

THE SURRENDER SCENE.

Sir David Beatty's Report.

PRESS BUREAU, Thursday, 2.20 p.m. The Secretary of the Admiralty makes the llowing announcement :—

never heard, while along the lines the signal ran to Admiral von Reuter :—

The German flag is to be hauled down at 5.57 to-day (Thursday and is not to be hoisted again

scuttled. Most of the ships did not stay where they had sunk. Those that were beached were removed almost immediately, the rest were salvaged over the next twenty years and by the twenty-first century there are the remains of only eight scuttled ships at Scapa Flow.

❖   ❖   ❖

A Cardiff MP unintentionally and unwittingly helped the Germans to build up their strong navy. Sir Edward Reed was one of a team of engineers who invented and designed a new type of warship that was being constructed by the Germans in 1913. The plans had been offered to the British as far back as 1884, but apart from a cursory acknowledgement the Admiralty had shown no interest. The Germans jumped at the chance nearly a decade later. The Reed vessel was faster than the successful Dreadnought class destroyer. More importantly the shape and design put forward by Reed presented a poor target for the enemy and could operate in all kinds of weather. Twenty destroyers of this type could be built for the cost of one Dreadnought. Prime Minister Asquith admitted in the Commons that the British had been offered the Reed design but did not explain why it had been rejected.

❖   ❖   ❖

American troops had bases in Cardiff with the American navy taking over the Angel Hotel which became known as USS *Chatinouka*. The first parade of American troops took place in the city on 31 July.

War or no war, Cardiff found time to honour Scott of the Antarctic and his crew. The Scott Lighthouse Clock was unveiled at Roath Park on 13 October (*see* p. 6).

1919

Postwar Riots

People from most countries in the world have settled in Cardiff, a city which can be proud of its record of integration. But there have been problems from time to time and none greater than in 1919 when major riots broke out. The clashes were sparked when troops and seamen returning from the First World War found that during the conflict immigrants had been brought in from the West Indies and Middle East to man ships and fill other vacancies. The bubble burst in June 1919 – verbal abuse turned to violence and shots rang out on Homfray Street. After two Black men were arrested, white youths set fire to their home. The fight started near the Labour Exchange in Custom House Street, and razors, sticks and stones as well as fists were used as weapons. A white man, Harold Smart, of Monmouth Street, Grangetown, died after having his throat cut in Caroline Street. A number of policemen were injured, and the contents of the home of one immigrant in Adam Street were ransacked by a group of white men. An American naval patrol came to the aid of the hard-pressed police and the fighting ended, only to be resumed over the next few days. Every policeman in the city was on duty throughout the disturbances and soldiers were standing by, but apart from the American naval patrol, had not been called in.

❖   ❖   ❖

The heir to the throne, Edward Prince of Wales, was made a Freeman of Cardiff on 26 June 1919. He had been invested as Prince of Wales at Caernarfon in 1911. In 1936 he succeeded King George V, but soon afterwards abdicated in order to marry an American divorcee, Wallis Simpson.

A number of Cardiff people were named in the April Fools honours list of 1919. For it was around 1 April that they received the official letters informing them of the intention to include them in the New Year's honours list for that year. The true list was made public at the end of April, having been delayed because the end of the First World War coincided with the time when honours were prepared. Sir William James Thomas, the coal-owner who was living in Cardiff, was made a baron. He endowed wards and beds in hospitals throughout South Wales, including Cardiff, and funded the Welsh School of Medicine which was established in Cardiff. Locals in the April list were Sir Herbert Cory, MP, Sir David Duncan, a director of the *Western Mail* and *Cardiff Times* and Sir Oswald Stoll, an Australian who had settled in Cardiff in the 1880s and founded the Empire Palace music hall in Queen Street.

Millions of people throughout the world died during the Spanish 'flu epidemic of 1918 and 1919. Hundreds of people in Cardiff were affected by the virus, which passed from animals to humans. The St John's Priory for Wales was founded in Cardiff on 1 March 1919.

1920

Anglicans Gain Independence

The battle for independence by the Anglican Church in Wales lasted for fifty years from 1870 to 1920. During the nineteenth century the Nonconformist denominations grew in Wales, and with the arrival of thousands of Irish refugees from the Great Famine of the 1840s, the Catholic Church was also growing fast. However, the Anglicans were, and still are, the largest single religious denomination in Wales.

The road to disestablishment was far from smooth, with violent clashes during the so-called 'Tithe Wars' when Welshmen objected to paying a tithe or tax to the Church of England. One of the most violent episodes occurred between 1886–90 when enraged Denbighshire farm labourers engaged in running battles with the local police and troops were brought in to protect the tithe collectors.

An Anti-Tithe League was formed to campaign across the country, and in south Caernarfonshire its secretary was a young solicitor, David Lloyd George, the future Prime Minister and Freeman of Cardiff. As a Nonconformist and politician, he did as much as, if not more than most to secure disestablishment for Welsh Anglicans.

Archbishops in England are appointed by the Queen, but in Wales they are elected by the Bench of Bishops. The first Archbishop of Wales was Alfred George Edwards, of St Asaph, who reigned from 1920 to 1934.

An insight into the Bay area of Cardiff when the Tiger had some teeth was given in a court case in the *South Wales Echo* in January 1920. The city magistrates were told of a police raid on an opium den at 100 Bute Street. Five Chinese men were arrested and charged with smoking and being in possession of the drug. The ringleader was fined £10 and the other four were fined £5 each after their defence counsel told the court they could not understand why they should be punished for enjoying their hobby. 'They have dreams of celestial paradise,' said their solicitor.

❖   ❖   ❖

In a year when motor buses were first introduced in Cardiff, the Splott Ward elected Rhoda Parker the city's first woman councillor, Cardiff City Football Club joined the Football League, and archaeologists at Cardiff Castle dug up relics from the past. Supervised by the Marquess of Bute they found a number of human skeletons, coins and pottery near the old Roman road, close to the castle keep.

Motor buses started operating in Cardiff in 1920.

1921

Blue-blooded Archbishop

Francis Mostyn was transferred to the Archdiocese of Cardiff from the Wrexham-based Menevia Diocese which he had founded after being made a bishop in 1895. He was enthroned Archbishop of Cardiff in the city's St David's Cathedral, on the Feast of St Joseph, 19 March 1921. Mostyn was a blue-blooded Catholic and the first post-Reformation leader of the Catholic Church in Wales to be actually born in the Principality. He was a member of the hierarchy for a total of forty-four years, eighteen of which were in Cardiff. It is a record which is not likely to be beaten now that bishops are expected to retire at the age of 75.

Mostyn's appointment to Cardiff was widely acclaimed, not least by the Liberal Prime Minister David Lloyd George, who was invited to the enthronement at St David's Cathedral but was unable to attend the ceremony because of a rail strike.

Before his death in 1939, Archbishop Mostyn was the driving force behind 1 March being adopted as St David's Day: 'The Irish rightly celebrate St Patrick's Day and we should salute St David, the Patron of Wales,' he said. Mostyn also composed the hymn to Great St David that is sung with gusto around the feast-day.

Buried at St Mary's churchyard in Whitchurch, Cardiff, is Charles Burley Ward, the last man to receive the Victoria Cross from Queen Victoria herself. He died on 30 December 1921, after leaving the army and retiring to Cardiff.

Charles Ward, who was born in Leeds, was 22 years old and a private in the 2nd Battalion of the King's Own Yorkshire Light Infantry when he was awarded the VC for bravery during the Boer War in South Africa. On 26 June 1900, at Lindley, South Africa, a group from Ward's regiment was surrounded on three sides by about 500 Boers and most of the British contingent were either killed or wounded. Private Ward volunteered to take a message asking for reinforcements to the signalling post about 150 yards away. Although it seemed certain that he would be shot, he managed to get across through a storm of bullets. Having delivered his message, he returned to his commanding officer across the fire-swept ground, and was severely wounded, but his gallant action saved the post from capture.

For more than sixty years Ward laid in an unmarked grave at Whitchurch, but in 1986, David Clarke, a verger of the church and secretary of the Glamorgan Family History Society, identified the grave. John O'Sullivan, co-author of this book, with the help of the Earl Haig British Legion Club at Whitchurch and The King's Own Yorkshire Light Infantry, arranged for a headstone to be placed on the grave. Ward's son and daughters were among those who attended the ceremony in 1986, when Pontlottyn-born Edward Chapman, VC, unveiled the headstone.

The Trades Union Congress chose Cardiff for the first time to host its annual general meeting in 1921, the year that the Dominions Building and Arcade was completed in Queen Street and the 3,000-seat Capital Cinema, the largest purpose-built cinema in Britain at the time, opened in Queen Street on Boxing Day. The University of Wales Press was established on 21 November, and Glamorgan played their first cricket match at the Cardiff Arms Park on 18, 19 and 20 May. Glamorgan won by twenty-three runs.

1922

First Broadcast

The first regular broadcasts were made from Cardiff 1923, but a Yorkshireman, Garforth Mortimer, who adopted the city as his home, claimed to be the first musician to take to the airwaves. He was invited to take part in an experiment from a first-floor shop to the left of the St Mary Street entrance to Cardiff market. Before his death in the late 1970s, he told John O'Sullivan what happened: 'I was asked to play the violin in front of a microphone. I learnt later that the performance had been heard by an invited audience who sat at the Cory Hall more than a half a mile away. They were each wearing headphones and clearly heard me play Garforth's Sunday Night concerts at the Park Hall were some of the most popular forms of entertainment in Cardiff for four decades.' He was also a leading Rotarian, and his wife, to whom he was married for more than seventy years, was a founder of the Inner Wheel Club.

Mortimer was leader of the orchestra that played for the silent films at the Park Hall Cinema in Cardiff, which opened on 24 September 1923. In a radio talk he gave in 1928, he told of the sensation that another musician had caused when he was selecting music for a biblical silent film. As Moses parted the Red Sea the orchestra struck up with 'A Life on the Ocean Wave'!

Solicitor Charles Hallinan had two reasons to celebrate in 1922. He was elected to the City Council for the first time and his son Lincoln was born. Both men became councillors and aldermen; both were elected lord mayors of the city; both were knighted by the Queen and both were made Papal Knights.

Alderman Sir Charles Hallinan and son Alderman Lincoln Hallinan following the elevation of Sir Charles to Cardiff City Council's aldermanic bench.

Also born in 1922 was Ken Hollyman, who became an outstanding half-back for Cardiff City and who was credited with having the longest throw-in of any footballer in Britain. He was also a star baseball player.

The suburbs of Llanishen and the old city of Llandaff became part of the City of Cardiff following boundary changes in 1922. Llandaff had no Royal Charter but had been a city for many centuries by virtue of having a cathedral. The Earl of Plymouth donated 22 acres of the Plymouth Great Wood to Cardiff in 1922, the year that Bute Docks Railway, Taff Vale Railway and Cardiff Railway were sold to the Great Western Railway Company.

Smith Junior Nautical College, where hundreds of naval officers were trained, was founded on 31 July. At the end of the century the college was demolished and redeveloped for residential purposes, known as Reardon Smith Court. Splott Baths opened on 14 August 1922.

1923

First Labour MP

When Arthur Henderson was elected for Cardiff South in December 1923 with a majority of less than 500, he became the first Labour member for the city, which twenty-two years later elected Jim Callaghan for the same constituency. Callaghan went on to become Chancellor of the Exchequer, Home Secretary and Prime Minister. Henderson gained the seat from the Conservative John Cory. It is believed that men who had returned from the war and women who had been given the vote for the first time in 1918 backed Labour at a time when there was high unemployment and rising food prices. Henderson's father, also called Arthur, was one of the founders of the Labour Party and had been leader on two occasions, in 1908 and 1914. The 1923 General Election was notable for other reasons: the future Labour Prime Minister Ramsay MacDonald was elected MP for Aberavon and Winston Churchill lost his seat in Leicester.

St Illtyd's College opened on 23 January 1923 on the site of a University Settlement in Courtney Road, which had been used for an experiment in adult education. The new college was mainly staffed by the De La Salle brothers, who went on to serve education in the city for seventy-four years. During that time more than seventy former pupils were ordained for the teaching order or for the priesthood. The centre of the college was destroyed by a German bomb on the night of 2 March 1941. The school continued to function in what was left of the premises.

The first radio station was established in 1923 and started broadcasting from Castle Street, Cardiff on 1 March. The first Welsh-language programme was broadcast on 8 November. This was also the year that Cardiff Infirmary became Cardiff Royal Infirmary and when reconstruction work started on Cardiff Castle, with the North Gate being built in Roman style.

1924

Football Olympian

The blockbuster film *Chariots of Fire* told the story of the fates of British athletes, especially the runners Harold Abrahams and Eric Liddel, in the 1924 Olympic Games in Paris. Had the plot included the Olympic soccer tournament, the spotlight could have shone on Cardiff City's George Latham, who took time off from Ninian Park to coach the British team at the Paris Games. Latham, who is featured in the Hall of Fame at St Fagans Museum of Life, coached Cardiff City FC during their greatest period of success between 1911 and 1936. They won the FA Cup in 1927 and only missed out on the League Championship in 1922/23 by goal difference. As a player Latham appeared for Wrexham, Liverpool, Southport and Cardiff City, and played twelve times for Wales.

The Welch Regiment Memorial was dedicated at Llandaff Cathedral on 19 July 1924, and the BBC opened their studio in Park Place on 17 March. Shortly afterwards the first Welsh-language radio play, *Y Pwyllgor* ('The Committee'), was broadcast. The widening of Duke Street, in front of Cardiff Castle, took place in June of this year.

The first Taff Swim took place from Canton Bridge to Clarence Road Bridge in 1924. It moved to Roath Park in 1931, when Canton Bridge was widened.

1925

Peerless Jim

The most famous son of Newtown, Cardiff, boxer 'Peerless' Jim Driscoll, died on 30 January 1925 at the age of 44. More than 100,000 people lined the route for the funeral procession of the man who sixteen years earlier gave up the chance of fighting for the featherweight championship of the world to take part in an exhibition bout at the Park Hall in aid of Nazareth House.

The Royal Oak, in Newport Road, is a shrine to 'Peerless' Jim Driscoll (right). The former landlady, his great-niece Kitty Flynn, is seen showing Jim's Lonsdale Belt to actor Michael Hewson, who played Jim in a play written by Tim Green (centre).

The funeral took place on 3 February 1925. Outside Cardiff Castle the coffin was placed on a gun carriage and an army band played solemn music as members of the 2nd Battalion of the Welch Regiment paid their tribute. The graveside service was conducted by Fr Grieshaber, wearing vestments paid for by Peerless Jim. The last post was sounded by an army bugler, and rifle shots were fired over the grave.

Peerless Jim worked in the composing room of the old *Evening Express*, which had its offices at the Monument end of St Mary Street, Cardiff. He acquired his boxing skills in the fairground booths run by the infamous Jack Scarott. At the age of 17 Jim was earning a sovereign a week from boxing. Scarott added a silver crown to each purse by tying the teenager's hands behind his back and offering a gold sovereign to anyone who could hit the courageous Driscoll on the nose inside a minute. The money was safe.

Driscoll won more than fifty professional fights in Britain before going to the United States, where he crowned his achievements in 1909 by out-boxing the world featherweight champion Abe Atell in a no-decision contest. But the hardbitten American boxing writers unanimously voted Driscoll as the winner and gave him the accolade of 'Peerless Jim', a tribute to his skilful left hand. Arrangements were being made for a rematch when the title would have been at stake, but Peerless Jim stunned the boxing world by opting to go home to raise money for the orphans being cared for by the Sisters of Nazareth at their house on the corner of Colum Road and North Road, Cardiff. Wales has rarely given a greater welcome to one of its sporting heroes than that given to Driscoll as he left Cardiff General station, surrounded by thousands of fans. He was carried shoulder high through the cheering throng to his home in Newtown.

The First World War deprived him of a chance of further world championship bouts. He joined the army and belonged to a famous khaki boxing squad that included Bombardier Billy Wells, Pat O'Keefe, Johnny Basham, Dick Smith, Captain Bruce Logan and the 'Mighty Atom', Jimmy Wilde. The end of his boxing career came at the National Sporting Club in London in October 1921, when his heartbroken seconds threw in the towel after Jim had been battered for sixteen rounds by the 'Little Assassin', Charles Ledoux, from France. Jim Driscoll died at the Duke of Edinburgh Hotel, where he was landlord, on the corner of Ellen Street, the street where he was born and raised. The headline in a national boxing magazine proclaimed 'THE KING IS DEAD'.

The headstone on Jim's grave was paid for by the Sisters of Nazareth, who posthumously gave him the title which he had sacrificed for them: 'OF YOUR CHARITY PRAY FOR THE SOUL OF JIM DRISCOLL, RETIRED FEATHERWEIGHT CHAMPION OF THE WORLD.'

In 1997 a statue of Peerless Jim was erected near the site of the former Central Boys Club where he used to train. More than seventy years after his death, Jim's nephew, Bernard Rowlands, of Penarth, presented items connected with Driscoll to the Welsh Hall of Fame, at the Museum of Welsh Life, St Fagans. They included a pair of boxing gloves, presented to Driscoll by Abe Atell.

Cardiff City reached the final of the FA Cup for the first time in 1925 but lost 1–0 to Sheffield United at Wembley.

On 31 May that year the first Welsh-language religious broadcast came from Tabernacle Welsh Baptist Church in The Hayes, Cardiff, a landmark occasion which echoed the glorious days of the Nonconformist Revival around the turn of the nineteenth and twentieth centuries. One wonders what world reaction would have been had radio or even television broadcast the Revival services, the words of the outstanding Welsh preachers and wonderful hymns.

The Tower of St Albans Church, Splott, collapsed during a gale on 9 February. It could have provided a good subject for students of the Welsh School of Architecture, which was founded in Cardiff that year. Coinciding with the twentieth anniversary of Cardiff as a city, William Nicholls, a benefactor of the Royal Infirmary, donated his home at St Mellons to be used as a convalescent home.

Three men who contributed much to the city were born that year: Stewart Williams, whose illustrated histories have made sure that 'Cardiff Yesterday' will be known to future generations; comedian, entertainer and pantomime promoter Stan Stennett, whose contribution to stage and screen put smiles on generations of faces; and full-back Ron Stitfall, who was a favourite with Cardiff and Welsh soccer fans in the winning days of the 1950s.

1926

General Strike

Most of Britain ground to a halt during May 1926 after the Trades Union Congress called a general strike in support of the fight for better pay and conditions by the miners. The order went out to trade unionists working on the railways, the buses and trams, seamen and dockers, printers, and steel and factory workers. The *South Wales Echo* reported on 23 May that Cardiff started walking after tram crews joined the strike. The big trek to the heart of the city and dockyards started at daybreak when, although a few private buses were running, the pavements echoed to the sound of thousands of feet. Rusty, decrepit old bicycles that had long forgotten the road were brought out again, and people owning a tandem picked up a second rider on the way.

The government ordered troops to Cardiff after rioting broke out in St John Square when a crowd of strikers tried to overturn a Ford car that was plying for hire. Several people were injured and one man was taken to hospital. The next day 45-year-old William Walsh appeared before Cardiff magistrates accused of trying to prevent the proper working of a vehicle and assaulting police constable John Gale. The court was told that Walsh had thrown stones and tried to stop a Cardiff Corporation bus. He was sentenced to two months' hard labour. Two other men were jailed for short terms with hard labour for trying to prevent volunteers manning a Corporation bus. The accused appeared in court with their heads swathed in bandages.

The *Echo* printers were on strike, but the usual broadsheet newspaper came out in tabloid form, with women typists operating the printing machines.

Cardiff's Lord Mayor, Alderman William Francis, was given a standing ovation in the council chamber for recruiting volunteers to keep public services operating. Alderman W.H. Pethybridge said the Council would not be ruled by a Soviet Committee in London. Councillor H. Hiles disapproved of the Lord Mayor's action, especially his promise to give a permanent job to every volunteer. Hiles described this as an act of intimidation of the men who had had the courage to stand up for what they thought was right and proper.

The strike began to crumble in Cardiff when tramway men were told they would lose their jobs unless they returned to work within twenty-four hours. More than 150 men reported to the Clare Road tram depot, and most of the others reported that evening or the next day. Other strikers, mainly railwaymen, set up picket lines but failed to stop the return to work.

An airship designed and built by Ernest Willows.

The General Strike ended on 12 May after Sir Herbert Samuel had proposed a formula acceptable to the TUC, one of the main clauses being the establishment of a National Wages Board. One part of Cardiff has an historic link with the General Strike: Hailey Park in Llandaff North opened on 1 May 1926, just as the strike was starting.

Ernest Willows, the Cardiff man who is acknowledged as the father of the British airship, died tragically in a ballooning accident at a flower show in Kempton, Bedfordshire, on 3 August 1926. His death came sixty years after he caused a sensation by piloting his airship *City of Cardiff* from Pengam Airport across the Bristol Channel to Minehead in Somerset on 6 August 1910. In November that year he piloted the airship from England to France. Willows' airships, assembled in a hangar in Westgate Street, Cardiff, were used by the Royal Navy and commercial firms. Captain Willows is buried in Cathays Cemetery, Cardiff, but his greatest monument is Willows High School, Willows Avenue, Tremorfa.

1927

Cup of Joy

Rugby may be a religion in Wales, but the greatest day in Welsh sporting history was 25 April 1927, when, in front of a 91,000 crowd, Cardiff City won the FA Cup – the only team to take the coveted trophy out of England. The City, who were beaten finalists to Sheffield United two years earlier, beat the mighty Arsenal by the only goal of the match, scored fifteen minutes from time. The goal, scored by Hughie

Ferguson, was blamed on the Arsenal goalkeeper, Dan Lewis, who hailed from Maerdy, in the Rhondda. Lewis seemed to have caught the ball but it spun out of his hands into the net. City's captain Fred Keenor collected the cup from King George V, who only four days earlier had opened the National Museum of Wales in Cardiff. Before the match he was so impressed with the singing of the thousands of Welsh fans that he called for an encore of 'Abide with Me'. Among those at the match were David Lloyd George, Winston Churchill and the Lord Mayor of Cardiff.

When the team returned to Cardiff two days later, thousands turned out to see the players tour the decorated streets of the city in an open-top bus. It was a glorious day for Cardiff and for Welsh sport, and especially for the people who had failed to get a ticket for Wembley and had to be content with listening to a radio commentary – an innovation that had been introduced only two months earlier when Wales played Ireland at rugby.

This was the year that Lord Jack Brooks was born. He became a city councillor and was made a life peer after acting as election agent to James Callaghan for many years.

The River Ely overflowed on 3 November 1927, allowing Billy the Seal to leave her pool at Victoria Park and go for her legendary swim along Cowbridge Road East. There was a total eclipse of the sun in June of that year and a blizzard on Christmas Day.

1928

O Danny Boy

On a cold January night in 1928, 10,000 people stood outside Cardiff Prison praying in vain for a miracle to save the lives of two convicted murderers who were spending their last hours in the death cell.

Throughout the night the mainly Catholic crowd recited the rosary and sang hymns, and as dawn broke on 27 January they sang 'Faith of Our Fathers' and 'Danny Boy' in the hope that their voices would carry through the tall thick walls of the prison to the condemned men. At 8 a.m. the prison bell tolled to tell the weeping men, women and children that Danny Driscoll and Edward 'Titch' Rowlands had been hanged by the public executioner Thomas Pierrepoint for the murder of Dai Lewis, a rugby player and professional boxer. Driscoll's four brothers were the first to read the notice of the hanging when it was placed on the prison door.

Dai Lewis died in a street fight near the entrance to the Wyndham Arcade, in St Mary Street, Cardiff, on 29 September 1927. His throat had been cut – not by Driscoll or Titch Rowlands, but by Rowlands' younger brother, John, who had been

Part of the crowd outside Cardiff Prison when Danny Driscoll and Titch Rowlands were executed in 1928.

declared insane and sent to Broadmoor. Titch Rowlands was thought to have been involved in a plot to maim, but not murder Lewis, who is believed to have made the mistake of trying to take over a protection racket run by the Rowlands at Ely Racecourse. He was drinking in a nearby pub when the fatal attack took place.

Canon Daniel Hannon, administrator of St David's Cathedral and a future Bishop of Menevia, heard Driscoll's last confession. He said at Mass at the cathedral later that morning: 'They hanged an innocent man at Cardiff jail this morning . . .' He was not the only one of that opinion. On the eve of the execution, two members of the jury who had found Driscoll guilty, travelled to London with a petition signed by themselves and six other jurymen begging for mercy for Driscoll. The acting Home Secretary, Sir Austen Chamberlain, rejected their plea. More than 500,000 people throughout Britain had signed petitions calling for Driscoll to be saved from the gallows; Liverpool dockers called for a national strike, and prayers were offered in Catholic churches throughout Britain and Ireland.

On the eve of his execution, Driscoll drank a bottle of port and played cards with the warder who was guarding him. As he walked to the gallows, he joked, 'They've given us a good day for it.'

In the 1980s, the warder's daughter, who lived at Bridgend, said her father had told her that he was convinced of Driscoll's innocence. The feeling at the time of his execution was that the authorities wanted to make an example of Driscoll and Titch Rowlands as a warning to race gangs who were operating throughout Britain.

Had the two men not been tried they would no doubt have joined the crowds at the first greyhound races and speedway meetings that were held at the Sloper Road track from that year. They might even have gone along to the Plaza Cinema, in North Road, which opened its doors on 12 March, though it is doubtful if they would have bothered to attend the first concert by the National Orchestra of Wales, conducted by Henry Wood, at the City Hall on 12 April, or bothered to join the new Gabalfa Library, which was launched on 25 April.

In 2004 the prison authorities agreed to the six bodies of hanged men, including Driscoll and Rowlands, to be exhumed and buried in public cemeteries. At the time Cardiff solicitor Bernard de Maid was seeking a posthumous pardon for Driscoll. Although there was little public sympathy for Rowlands, his broken-hearted wife begged in vain for mercy for her husband, whose brother was the killer. If a posthumous pardon is granted for Driscoll then Rowlands may be granted the same right.

Major changes took place in the newspaper industry in Cardiff when David Duncan and family sold the *South Wales Daily News* to the *Western Mail*, which had been launched in Cardiff in 1869. On 17 August 1928, the *Western Mail* paid £525,000 for the *Daily News* only to close it down a week later. The *Evening Express* continued for another two years before it, too, closed, leaving the evening market free for the *South Wales Echo*, which became recognised as one of the best regional newspapers in Britain. The Kemsley family, which had its roots in Merthyr, bought the *Western Mail* and *Echo* in 1936.

The Welsh National War Memorial was unveiled on 12 June by the Prince of Wales in Cathays Park, with much of the work on the monument being carried out by the long-established Cardiff monumental masons Mossfords. There was heavy snow in February, and a cyclone damaged hundreds of houses in Cardiff in November 1928, the year that Rhymney station, a twin of Queen Street station, was closed down.

The USS *George Washington*, believed to be the largest liner to dock in Cardiff, arrived on 29 July.

1929

Off to Canada

When the passenger liner *Montrose* docked at Cardiff in April 1929, it was possible for people to travel steerage to Canada for £10. More liners came sailed between Cardiff and Canada over the next few years and the Welsh port was being hailed as a new Liverpool. But with high unemployment and the depression of the 1930s, the Cardiff trade ceased.

Gus Risman, acclaimed as one of the greatest centre-three-quarters of all time, signed for Salford Rugby League side for the princely sum of £77 on 31 January 1929. He was the 17-year-old son of Latvian parents who had settled in Cardiff. He

went on to play for Wales eighteen times between 1931 and 1945; for Great Britain seventeen times between 1932 and 1946. Gus (left) toured Australia three times, captaining the side in nine test matches.

This was the year that all three Cardiff constituencies returned Labour MPs and when the Board of Guardians was abolished. Cardiff-born Flight Lieutenant Jenkins was the navigator of the first non-stop flight from Britain to India. Sadly he later died when a plane carrying him from South Africa crashed. The first talking picture, *The Jazz Singer*, starring Al Jolson, was shown at the Queens Cinema in Queen Street on 11 March. Gales and torrential rain caused part of the Bute Street rail embankment to collapse in November, and the storms continued through to December. The first Wales v England Speedway meeting was held at Sloper Road on 17 July.

The War Memorial, which was established in Cathays Park in 1929.

1930

Cardiff's Benefactor

A statue of the 3rd Marquess of Bute was unveiled, in Friary Gardens, Cardiff, in 1930. John Patrick Crichton-Stuart was not just the 3rd Marquess of Bute but also Earl of Windsor and Baron Cardiff. He was one of the richest men in the world when he celebrated his twenty-first birthday in 1868, shortly after which he embraced the Catholic faith. He was to be the greatest benefactor to the Catholic cause in Cardiff.

His father, the 2nd Marquess, was the man who turned Cardiff into a major port. He had made huge speculative investments in the burgeoning industries of South Wales during the early nineteenth century and laid the foundations of the export system that would change Cardiff from a modest market town into one of the world's greatest industrial ports. The 3rd Marquess was born at Mountstuart House, Isle of Bute, Scotland, on 16 September 1847 and was only six months old when his father died at the age of 54 at Cardiff Castle, in the room later converted into the Lady Chapel.

The 3rd Marquess was described as a serious but priggish young man when he first came to Cardiff in the summer of 1868. He marked his twenty-first birthday by going on a cruise to Russia, via the North Sea. But Cardiff celebrated the birthday with a week of festivities and, as reported in the *Cardiff Times*, was in state of excitement such as had never before been witnessed. Events included illuminations, ox-roasts and fireworks, and a grand ball, culminating with the arrival by yacht of Bute. He drove in a procession through the decorated streets of the town.

His income at the time was said to be around £300,000 a year, part of which was to be spent on rebuilding Cardiff Castle and building Castell Coch, at Tongwynlais. Both projects were entrusted to the architect William Burges. Bute married the Hon. Gwendoline FitzAlan Howard, daughter of the Earl of Glossop, at Brompton Oratory. The couple honeymooned in Cardiff.

To mark their silver wedding in 1897, the Marquess and Marchioness of Bute set up a £1,000 trust fund to provide a dowry for a girl of the poorer classes in Cardiff whose marriage might be impeded by the want of such a sum. One of the conditions laid down was that the bride and groom should have the first eleven verses of the second chapter of the Gospel of St John read to them to remind them of the story of the marriage feast in Cana when Christ performed his first miracle by turning water into wine.

The Butes were not the only benefactors to Cardiff. For example, in 1930 former Lord Mayor Alderman R.G. Hill-Snook donated 26 acres of land at the Wenallt to the City.

The genius who created the Daleks, the robot monsters of the *Dr Who* television series, was born in Cardiff on 8 August 1930. He was science-fiction writer Terry Nation, who also created *Blake's Seven* and *Survivors*. Nation started in the comedy

field and was encouraged by the *Goon Show*'s Spike Milligan, who bought one of his sketches in 1965. Nation wrote many of the sketches made famous by comedian Tony Hancock in the 1960s before being commissioned by the BBC to write for the *Dr Who* series. Terry Nation died in Los Angeles on 9 March 1997. In 2004 the *Dr Who* series was relaunched by the BBC, and appropriately it was filmed in Nation's home city of Cardiff.

Terry Nation, the Cardiff-born scriptwriter, is pictured here with his daughter Rebecca and one of his most famous creations – a Dalek. Nation was responsible for a host of major television series including *The Avengers*, *The Saint* and *The Persuaders*.

A student named Pugh from Aberystwyth University was called to order at a conference hosted by the Liberals at Cardiff University. He had dared to address the conference, which was discussing Home Rule for Wales, in the Welsh language! The conference also called for a Board of Education for Wales, and this is the year when Cathays High School for Boys and Girls and Heathfield House Catholic School for Girls opened in Cardiff.

1931

A True Champion

A Cardiff man took the amateur boxing world by storm in 1931 when, in just fifty days, he won both the British heavyweight and light-heavyweight titles. Jack Petersen turned professional in the same year and won his first twenty-six bouts in twenty-six months – collecting the British and Empire titles on the way. He lost his first professional fight – and his titles – when he was beaten on points by Len Harvey in November 1933. He regained his titles seven months later when he knocked out Harvey in the second round. Petersen lost his crowns when he was knocked out by Ben Ford in the third round in 1936 and hung up his gloves the following year. He went on to become President of the Welsh area council of the British Boxing Board of

Welsh boxer Jack Petersen (left) engages in sparring practice, 1931.

Control, served on the Sports Council for Wales and became the first chairman of the Welsh Ex-boxers Association. He was awarded an OBE in 1978 and died in November 1990; his grave is on the Heritage Trail at Cathays Cemetery.

The annual Taff Swim, which had been held down river for many years, moved to Roath Park Lake in July 1931. More than 10,000 spectators lined the lake to watch swimmers from many parts of the country take part in the event, which included races for men and women. Channel swimmer Ted Temme, of the Plaistow United Club, was a hot favourite to win the men's race. However, although he touched first, he finished in the wrong place. Arthur Watt, from West Ham, was declared the winner.

The Welsh School of Medicine obtained its Royal Charter in 1931, the year that the 4th Marquess of Bute officially opened Canton Bridge. The 'History of Cardiff' was told in a two-day pageant at the Castle in June and the first air pageant was held at Pengam Airport in October.

Sensational evidence of conditions in refreshment houses in the docks district of Cardiff was given by Chief Constable James Wilson to a Parliamentary Commission on licensing in January 1931. He described the food and equipment in the cafés as of doubtful quality and said the premises were frequented by women of low morality. Heavy penalties imposed by the courts were no deterrent. Wilson complained that he had no power to enforce the cafés to close at reasonable hours and said the mingling of the sexes had produced a major social problem in Cardiff. About 400 babies had been born of mixed White and non-White parents. He worried about the amount of methylated spirits being served and drunk in the cafés, and believed that the Sunday opening of public houses would help to alleviate some of the problems.

1932

Hungry Thirties

This was the decade when families throughout Britain were struggling to survive; the years when grown men – including First World War veterans – wept as they begged the local Guardians to give them a pittance of a grant to help feed their wives and children, and were forced to queue at soup kitchens set up by churches and charities. They were the years when men's hearts were broken because their benefit had been docked on account of the two shillings that a son had earned delivering newspapers.

It was against this background that 2,500 hunger marchers from all over Britain set off for London. Nearly 400 marchers, led by Whitchurch-born leading communist Will Paynter, left Cardiff on 14 October 1932. They marched to London, begging for money and food en route. They joined the other marchers who presented a petition to Parliament on 1 November, protesting against the abolition of the hated Means Test and Anomalies Act, fearing that the system would be replaced by an even less favourable one. The protest was also against proposed cuts in social services, and a planned 10 per cent reduction in unemployment benefit.

In 1934 the Unemployment Insurance Bill came into force. This meant that rates were set at a national level and could not be decided locally. In February 1934 another nationwide hunger march took place, protesting against this Bill, with the marchers from the Valleys again passing through Cardiff on their way to London. Among the supporters of that march was Nye Bevan, the Labour MP, who in the late 1940s was the architect of the National Health Service.

The last major hunger march to leave South Wales and to pass through Cardiff took place in October 1936, with 504 marchers involved. The march was backed not only by the Labour Party and local councils but also by church and chapel leaders. Many activists were missing from that march as they had gone to Spain to fight fascist leader General Franco.

❖   ❖   ❖

Few people have made a greater impact on the nuclear-fuel industry in Britain than Walter Marshall, who was born in Cardiff in 1932. After leaving St Illtyd's College he obtained his doctorate in solid-state physics at the University of Birmingham. He joined the Atomic Energy Research Establishment and became Chief Scientific Adviser to the Energy Minister Tony Benn. The second generation of Britain's gas-cooled nuclear power stations was proving a disaster. Marshall was an advocate of the American pressurised-water system, but his clashes with the Minister led Benn's team to describe the Cardiff man as a self-satisfied, pompous man with poor political judgement. Abandoned by Benn, Marshall returned to Harwell.

When Margaret Thatcher was elected Prime Minister in 1979, she was impressed by the way in which Marshall improved Harwell's efficiency. Marshall was knighted and put in charge of the Central Electricity Generating Board, with an order to promote nuclear power. He was credited with keeping the lights burning during the miners' strike in the 1980s and was rewarded by being elevated to the House of Lords. It was not long before he disagreed with the Thatcher Government, which privatised the industry, ignoring his advice that only by keeping the CEGB together could nuclear power be successfully pursued.

CEGB Chairman Lord Walter Marshall and Baroness Hopper stand beneath one of the wind turbines being tested at Carmarthen Bay Power Station, Burryport, 19 October 1988.

With his electrical power empire privatised Lord Marshall's rule was over. His one wish is that he will be remembered as the man who introduced the Sizewell B Power Station in Suffolk, the only one built in Britain to the design he championed.

❖   ❖   ❖

There was no rainfall recorded during the whole month of February in 1932, the year that Valerie Davies of Cardiff won a bronze medal, finishing third in the 100-metres backstroke in the Olympic Games in Los Angeles, in a time of 1 minute 22.5

seconds. It was the year a service was inaugurated between Pengam Airport, Cardiff, and Bristol; the year when the National Museum East Wing and the Reardon Smith Theatre opened; when Glamorgan County Hall was extended; when the Grand Theatre in Westgate Street was closed and Cardiff Little Theatre founded.

1933

University Celebrates

By the twenty-first century there was an estimated 14,000 students studying in Cardiff, most of them at the university that celebrated its fiftieth anniversary with a garden party at the Castle in 1933. The university can trace its roots back to 1881 when a report by Lord Aberdare recommended setting up universities in North and South Wales to complement the University College of Wales, then based at Aberystwyth. Following a public appeal that raised £37,000, the University College of South Wales and Monmouthshire opened in Cardiff on 24 October 1883, and was incorporated by Royal Charter the following year. Originally the college entered students for the examinations of the University of London. It celebrated its tenth birthday in 1893 by becoming one of the founding institutions of the University of Wales. In 1904 the first woman professor in the United Kingdom, Millicent McKenzie, was appointed in Cardiff. In June 1905, the year Cardiff was made a city, the Prince of Wales laid the foundation for the main university building in Cathays Park. As the city celebrated its anniversary, the college became Cardiff University, a title which many people believed was long overdue.

Despite the depression a number of projects were progressed in Cardiff, some of them under a scheme to provide work for the army of unemployed. Western Avenue was completed in 1933, but the planned Eastern Avenue did not open until nearly forty years later.

A sign that motor traffic was increasing in 1933 came when one-way streets were designated off St Mary Street. Spillers grain jetty was completed at Cardiff Docks, where many ships were laid up because of the lack of trade.

1934

Cardiff Catholics Protest Against Immoral Films

A protest movement that started in Cardiff quickly spread throughout the world and had a powerful effect on the contents of films made in Hollywood for the next twenty years. The Most Revd Francis Mostyn, who became Roman Catholic Archbishop of Cardiff in 1921, paid frequent visits to Rome. While he was there in 1934, Pope Pius XI asked him to campaign against what he described as the modern tendency towards immorality in public entertainment. When he returned to Wales, Mostyn founded the Cardiff Board of Catholic Action, the first organisation of its kind in the world. Within weeks it boasted more than 12,000 members and its first act was to declare war on immoral films. The *Welsh Catholic Times* reported that the move had created a mild sensation, particularly in the cinema industry where it was feared the movement for cleaner and better films would spread throughout Britain and overseas.

The Cardiff action group threatened that Catholics would boycott cinemas unless the adulation of the gangster and immoral and easy-divorce themes were eliminated. Cinema managers were asked not to show films that reflected on public morals or lowered the fundamental principles of religion. The pressure from Cardiff and from Catholics in America forced the cinema industry to set up a panel to vet cinema scripts for every film made from the mid-1930s to the 1950s.

Archbishop Francis Mostyn who led a campaign against immoral films.

When Mostyn celebrated the Golden Jubilee of his priesthood in 1934, the Earl of Dumfries called him the best-loved man in Wales. When he died from a sudden heart attack on 25 October 1939, the *South Wales Echo* described Mostyn as a great priest, a devoted son of Catholic Wales and one of the greatest churchmen of any creed that the Principality had produced. It is doubtful this view was shared by the giants in the cinema industry who, for two decades, had their work in America scrutinised by a board of censors chaired by a Jesuit priest as a result of the campaign launched by Mostyn in Cardiff.

❖　　❖　　❖

Cardiff boxers bantamweight Albert Barnes and flyweight Jackie Pottinger were among the medal winners at the Empire Games in London in 1934, winning silver and bronze respectively.

Medal-winning boxer Albert Barnes.

Valerie Davies, of Cardiff, won bronze in the 100-yards backstroke, in a time of 1 minute 15 seconds. Other Welsh silver medal winners were boxers J.D. Jones, flyweight, and Frank Taylor, lightweight. Tom Davies and Stan Weaver won bronze in the bowls pairs competition. Their success was a boost for the game back home where the Welsh Indoor Bowls Federation was founded in 1934. Two of Cardiff's greatest sportsmen, Rugby League ace Billy Boston and boxer Joe Erskine, were born in 1934.

The Lyne Grandstand was built at a cost of £20,000 and formally opened when Wales played England in 1934. England beat Wales by three tries (nine points) to nil. The Welsh captain, John Evans of Newport, was killed in action in North Africa in 1943. Two years earlier the Lyne Grandstand was destroyed when a parachute mine dropped on the Arms Park, causing considerable damage to the stands and terraces. It landed near the riverside goal posts and caused a crater 14ft deep and 50ft wide.

The modernisation of the Dowlais Works, East Moors, started in 1934, the year that Cardiff General station reopened after extensive reconstruction. Also during this year, the city's first traffic roundabout was created at the junction of Cardiff Road and Western Avenue.

1935

Murdered in Mongolia

Many famous journalists have worked for the *Western Mail and Echo* in Cardiff over the years, but perhaps none more famous than Gareth Jones, who was born in 1905, the year that Cardiff was created a city. During 1935 he was murdered by Chinese bandits in Mongolia. The articles he wrote for the *Western Mail* and other newspapers in the early 1930s revealed that famine was killing millions of people in Russia and Ukraine – a claim that was fervently denied by Joe Stalin's government.

Gareth, the son of Major Edgar Jones, headmaster of Barry Boys' Grammar School, had worked as an aide to former Prime Minister David Lloyd George before joining the *Western Mail*. Lloyd George was full of praise for the investigative journalist who had an 'unfailing knack of getting at things that mattered'. Decades after his death his writings are still being studied by academics across the world.

This was the year that Leckwith Bridge opened, giving a much welcomed alternative

Gareth Jones, the former *Western Mail* journalist and former secretary to David Lloyd George, is seen here with a Mongolian prince. It was his last interview before being captured and shot by Chinese bandits during 1935.

to Penarth Road, where the toll-gate was still charging motorists to use the route.

The first RAC Welsh rally started from Cardiff in July, and the following month the first pedestrian crossing was introduced in Queen Street, which was not pedestrianised in those days. The crossing was handy for people going to the newly opened Odeon Cinema. A fire in Cardiff market caused problems for traders and shoppers during Christmas week.

Two men who were to make an impact on society were born in 1935: Paul Flynn, a Labour MP for Newport, whose contribution to the House of Commons saw him named as a Backbencher of the Year, and Vincent Kane who became an outstanding broadcaster and television personality with BBC Wales. Shipowner William Reardon-Smith, who founded the college that carried his name, died in December 1935.

1936

Two New Freemen

A member of the landed gentry (the Earl of Plymouth) and a sculptor who was the son of a humble woodcarver were both made Freemen of Cardiff in 1936.

The sculptor was Sir William Goscombe John, who in 1882 studied with his father, who was a woodcarver at Cardiff Castle, under the direction of architect William Burges. The young Goscombe John also studied in London and Paris and won a gold medal and travelling scholarship in 1889. He worked under the internationally renowned sculptor Auguste Rodin in Paris, and was awarded another gold medal in 1901. He was knighted in 1911. His works, many of which can be seen at the National Museum and Galleries in Cardiff, include religious and poetic figures. Monuments created by him include the *Edward VII* in Liverpool and *Sir Arthur Sullivan* in St Paul's, London.

Mass demonstrations against unemployment were held in Cardiff in 1936, the year in which the first steel ingots were produced at East Moors Steelworks following a major modernisation, and Spillers Mill at Roath Dock was opened. It was also the year the first pedestrian crossing was laid in St Mary Street. Speedway racing ended at Sloper Road.

1937

Silver Screens and Civil War

Before the advent of the multiplex cinemas in the 1990s, Cardiff suburbs were well served by local silver screens. The Monico Cinema in Rhiwbina opened in April 1937 and was attracting good audiences up to 2002 when it was demolished to make way for new flats, which sold within hours of going on the market. Other cinemas that have closed down in Cardiff include The Plaza in North Road, which had to paint its roof black during the war as its white roof was considered too helpful to German bombers, and The Rialto, off Old Church Road, Whitchurch, among many others.

The first family-planning clinic opened in Cardiff, despite strong opposition from the local police. In January fire destroyed part of the grandstand at Ninian Park.

One of many cinemas that provided entertainment for the people of Cardiff was the Central Cinema, seen here in 1937.

In April 1937, as Spain was gripped by civil war, the Nationalist insurgents under General Franco announced a naval blockade of the Basque Country, with the aim of bringing a Republican stronghold to its knees. Franco had few ships to enforce the blockade, but the Royal Navy appeared willing to aid him by warning British vessels not to attempt to enter Bilbao.

There was a long tradition of trade between Cardiff and Bilbao, with steamers taking Welsh coal to Spain and returning with iron ore for the steelworks in Wales. After the shipping slump of the 1930s, the Spanish Civil War brought an increase in trade, as the elected Republican government offered to pay a premium to vessels prepared to take the risk of entering the war zone to deliver badly needed supplies. By 1937, eighteen steamers from South Wales were trading to Bilbao and other northern Spanish ports.

Four Cardiff vessels and their skippers hit the headlines as the blockade began to bite. They were all diverted by the Royal Navy into the southern French port of St Jean de Luz, where it was discovered that three had captains by the name of Jones. The Navy – and British reporters dispatched to the scene – distinguished them by their cargoes: Corn Cob Jones, Ham & Egg Jones and Potato Jones.

Captain David 'Potato' Jones became the first to attempt to run the blockade, on 15 April. On board his ship, the *Marie Llywellyn*, was a young Cardiff sailor called

Jimmy O'Brien, who later told the story of how the Royal Navy forced them – and their cargo of rotting potatoes – back into St Jean de Luz. Though he failed, his effort won him applause from the Opposition in the House of Commons.

Two days later, another Cardiff ship, the *Seven Seas Spray* left St Jean de Luz under cover of darkness, put out all her lights and headed for Bilbao. She was part owned by a Mr Pope, of the Seabank Hotel, Porthcawl, and skippered by Captain Bill Roberts of Penarth. There were six officers and what was described at the time as 'a cheerful coloured crew'. Also on board was the Captain's 20-year-old daughter, Florence, known as Fifi, who described their heroes' welcome in Bilbao in dispatches to the *News Chronicle* in London. They delivered a cargo of salt, ham, flour, beans and peas to the desperate population of the city.

While in the Basque Country, Fifi Roberts visited the ruins of Guernica, bombed by Hitler's Luftwaffe on 26 April 1937, and reported on the destruction for the British press. The *Seven Seas Spray* continued to trade along the coast of northern Spain until June 1937, when Bilbao fell to Franco's forces.

1938

Golden Games

All Wales cheered Cardiff-born Jim Alford who, when he was a member of Roath Harriers, won the gold medal for the mile at the Empire Games in Sydney in a then record time of 4 minutes 11.6 seconds. At the World University Games in Paris the previous year he won both the 800 and 1500-metre races. As a squadron leader pilot during the Second World War he won the Royal Air Force 880 and mile championships. He coached the Welsh athletes at the Empire Games in Cardiff in 1958 and later became the national coach to Rhodesia and Nyasaland (now Malawi). He also helped Britain's 4 × 1500-metre team break the world record. In Wales, Jim won eleven Welsh titles in a range of disciplines from the 440 yards to cross country. He coached numerous Welsh international stars, including Olympic and Commonwealth Games medal winners Ken Jones, Ron Jones and Nick Whitehead. Jim died in London at the age of 91 on 4 August 2004.

Jim Alford was not the only Cardiff man to win a gold medal at the 1938 British Empire Games. Denis Reardon, one of the other five members of the Welsh team, won gold in the boxing ring. Dinnie was a 20-year-old apprentice at the Curran works when he was called up to contest the middleweight division of the Games. He was fifth choice for Wales, but the four fighters rated above him could not get time off from their work.

Welsh swimmer Jeanne Greenland took silver in the women's backstroke in 1938, but Cardiff's Reg Braddick, who owned a bicycle shop in Broadway for decades, had to pull out of the cycling road race with a puncture when he was in contention for a medal.

Visitors to Cardiff in 1937 were Joseph P. Kennedy, the American Ambassador to Britain, together with his family, including John F. Kennedy, who twenty-three years later was elected President of the United States. Ambassador Kennedy was in Cardiff at the invitation of the Lord Mayor, Alderman Oswald Purnell, to attend the annual general meeting of the Saint Vincent DePaul Society. He attended High Mass at St David's Cathedral when the celebrant was Cardinal Wiseman. The Kennedys stayed at St Donat's Castle, in Vale of Glamorgan, a holiday retreat favoured by American VIPs, including the newspaper magnate Randolph Hurst.

With war clouds gathering over Europe, gas masks were issued to residents of Cardiff, ironically just as the Temple of Peace was opened in Cathays Park. The Welsh Board of Health Building, which later became part of the Welsh Office, also opened in Cathays Park. The first British night flights, from Cardiff to Weston, were inaugurated, and the Bute Estate sold a large piece of its land in the city to Western Ground Rents for £4.5 million.

1939

Ready for War

Cardiff was getting ready for the war against Germany, which was declared by Prime Minister Neville Chamberlain on 3 September 1939. Community air-raid shelters had been erected and gas masks issued to adults and children. There were even Mickey Mouse gas masks for younger children and incubator-type protection for babies. There were scenes similar to 1914 as sailors from all over South Wales boarded trains to take them to major Royal Navy bases. Families and friends sang on the crowded platforms. Recruits reported to Maindy Barracks to sign up for the army. As the war clouds gathered, 3,000 women volunteered in Cardiff to join the Auxiliary Territorial Service. The *South Wales Echo* published a Sunday edition for only the second time in its history. The previous occasion was in October 1914, when it looked as if the Allies were close to the victory that did not, in fact, come for another four years.

One of the most moving cartoons ever published in any newspaper appeared on the front page of the *South Wales Echo* on 11 November 1939 – Armistice Day. The cartoon, by J.C. Walker, was published just sixty-nine days after the start of the Second World War and showed a peace angel in prison, bound by a chain and a steel ball decorated with a German swastika. The caption read: 'It should have been her 21st birthday party.'

The death was announced in March 1939 of Gwyn Nicholls, who captained the Welsh team which defeated the All Blacks 3–0 in 1905, the year that Cardiff was made a city. Acclaimed the greatest three-quarter ever to don a Wales or Cardiff shirt, Gwyn, who was sixty-four when he died, was Captain of Wales from 1898 to 1908 and won a total of twenty-six caps. His name is remembered on the Gwyn Nicholls Memorial Gate, which has been a gateway to the Arms Park, the National Ground and the Millennium Stadium.

Another anniversary is worth remembering in 2005 – the 150th anniversary of the opening of Ely Racecourse, which attracted massive crowds during its eighty-four years' history. As Cardiff historian, author and racing expert Brian Lee records, the racecourse opened in 1855, a successor to a similar facility at Heath Park. The last meeting at Ely, known as the Ascot of Wales, was held on 27 April 1939, when Keith Piggot, father of Lester, won the last race on a horse called Grasshopper. Ely Leisure Centre was built on the racecourse and a housing estate was developed there in the early 1950s.

Tommy Farr (left) in action.

Just twenty-one months after his legendary fight in New York in which he lost a fifteen-round battle on points against World Heavyweight Champion Joe Louis, Welshman Tommy Farr entered the ring at Ninian Park on 17 May 1939. He beat Larry Gains, who retired after five rounds.

'Tonypandy Tommy' fought and won his first professional fight in 1926 – when he was only 12 years of age. He was one of the young Welsh boys who donned gloves in a bid to escape the poverty of the Valleys. Farr won 95 of the 179 fights he fought, and among the men he beat were former world champions Max Baer and Tommy Loughron. He retired in 1940 but made a comeback ten years later, winning eleven of the sixteen bouts he fought between 1950 and 1953.

The statue to Billy the Seal at Victoria Park, where he died in 1939.

Generations of children loved Billy the Seal, the main attraction in Victoria Park Zoo, and many tears were shed when the playful pet died in 1939.

1940

First Air Raid Victims

Cardiff suffered its first fatal casualties from air raids on 9 July 1940, when a lone bomber swooped over the docks and landed a direct hit on the *San Felipe*, which was carrying a cargo of timber. The bomb exploded in one of the holds and seven men were killed.

Tim O'Brien, a burly docker of David Street, Cardiff, went into the bomb-damaged, smoke-filled hold three times to bring out injured and dying men. Tim (right), who had carried a wounded solider 600 yards to safety in the First World War, was awarded an industrial medal for his bravery in Cardiff – many felt it should have been the George Cross. Later he was steward of the Glamorgan Wanderers Club, before he became landlord of the Royal Hotel at Cadoxton, Barry.

On 22 August 1940 five Cardiff firemen died while helping to fight burning oil tanks at Pembroke Dock, which had been bombed three days earlier. The fire was the biggest of the war in Wales and the Germans returned on a second day to machine-gun some of the firefighters. Home Office official Tom Breakstold told an inquest how the men were twenty feet in front of him at work with a fire jet. 'Suddenly, there was a large burst of flame which seemed to envelop them,' he said. 'The last I saw of them was when they were retreating from the huge tongues of flame which shot out from everywhere.'

Many people who lived in the area of Albany Road were the victims of a vicious raid on 3 September 1940 – exactly one year to the day after Britain declared war on Germany. Eleven people, including six children, were killed and thirty-five injured in that raid.

Some 864 high-explosive bombs and 2,410 incendiaries fell on South Wales in the autumn and winter of 1940, but this was only a grim rehearsal for the blitz which came with a vengeance to Cardiff when 1941 was only two days old.

One of the saddest incidents in the early days of the war involved the SS *City of Benares*, a liner that was torpedoed by a German U-boat in the Atlantic when it was taking ninety child evacuees to Canada, including a number from Cardiff. Seventy-seven children, five from Cardiff, were among the two hundred and forty-eight people who lost their lives after leaving Liverpool. Reports at the time concentrated on the survivors rather than the victims. The five Cardiff youngsters continued their trip to Canada aboard the vessel that rescued them.

Twenty-five paddle-steamers took part in Operation Dynamo, when an armada of little ships evacuated 338,236 men, mainly British servicemen, from Dunkirk between 27 May and 4 June 1940. Six of the steamers were P. and A. Campbell vessels that had been used for pleasure trips across the Bristol Channel for decades.

They were the *Devonia*, *Glen Avon*, *Glen Gower*, the *Plinlimmon* (also known as the *Cambria*) the *Snaefell* (which also used the name of *Waverley*) and *Westward-Ho*.

The *Glen Avon* made two crossings to rescue a total of 888 men from the beach near La Panine. It played a communications role at the time of the Normandy Landing, but was lost when caught in a storm in the Bay of the Seine off the French coast on 2 September 1944.

The *Snaefell* rescued 931 troops from the beaches. It was sunk off the River Tyne during an air raid on 5 July 1941. The *Glen Gower* brought 1,235 troops back to Britain from Dunkirk in three crossings. The *Plinlimmon* completed one trip from Dunkirk, landing 900 men at Margate. The *Westward-Ho* rescued and landed 1,686 men, including a large French contingent.

Operation Starfish was a master plan to fool enemy aircraft, and one of the people who made it successful was Ken Paterson, of Whitchurch, Cardiff. Ken's team was given the task of building dummy bases to draw enemy bombers away from legitimate targets. As Ken explained, they set up mock Spitfires on farms. His job was to press the buttons which set off smoke and fire drums and gave the Germans the impression they had scored direct hits. It is estimated that the plan made 5 per cent of air raids ineffective. But the Germans were not totally fooled. Legend has it that a German bomber dropped a wooden bomb on one of the false bases.

1941

Under Attack

Cardiff was attacked by 111 German bombers on the night of 2/3 January 1941 when a total of 115 tonnes of high explosives were dropped on the city. The 1941 raid started at 6.37 p.m. on 2 January and the all-clear did not sound until 4.50 a.m. on 3 January.

Shortly before eight o'clock All Saints Church in Llandaff North was destroyed by fire and provided a beacon for the Luftwaffe to target Llandaff Cathedral, which was badly damaged by a parachute mine. St Michael's College, Llandaff, was also hit as were houses in Prospect Drive, Ely Road and Fairwater Road. A total of 165 people were killed in the raid, and 168 suffered serious injuries. Another 240 needed treatment for minor injuries.

Ninety-five houses were totally destroyed, and 233 so badly damaged that they had to be demolished. A further 426 houses were declared uninhabitable, until repairs could be carried out. Hundreds of families had to be evacuated from their homes and looked after in schools and churches, which were turned into rest centres. Hundreds of children were evacuated from Cardiff to towns in the South Wales Valleys. Had the children stayed in Cardiff a few more weeks they may have seen King George VI and Queen Elizabeth, who paid a morale-boosting visit in February 1941. They were cheered in the streets and at Currans Works in the docks area.

When the siren sounded at 8.25 p.m. on 3 March 1941, it signalled the start of another major raid on Cardiff. Lansdowne Road School and Moorland Road School, at opposite ends of the city, were set on fire by incendiary bombs. But the chief target was the docks. A high-calibre bomb hit Mountstuart Dry Dock, damaging buildings but no ships. An incendiary bomb lodged in the entry gantry of Spillers Mill, causing dust explosions and seriously damaging plant and machinery. A total of forty-six people died in Cardiff that night.

This was the raid in which St. David's Roman Catholic Cathedral, in Charles Street, was gutted by fire bombs. People knelt in the street as Fr Patrick Creed carried the Blessed Sacrament 400 yards to St David's Hall, which was used as a pro-cathedral for the next eighteen years.

There was widespread destruction in Albany Road after an air raid in 1941.

Churchill visited Cardiff in April 1941. He toured the city in an open car, called at Cardiff Royal Infirmary, which had been bombed, and met the people of Grangetown and Riverside, who had suffered most in the air raid of 2 and 3 January 1941. In Neville Street he was handed a portrait of himself that had hung in the Conservative Club which had been destroyed in the raid.

RAF St Athan was a key base in the war against Germany, with more than 15,000 flight engineers being trained there. Hundreds of these were decorated for bravery, including Norman Jackson, who was awarded the VC for his attempt to save a burning bomber. In 1941 Rhoose Airport – later renamed Cardiff Airport – became a base for British fighter planes.

Around this time Cardiff lost one of its popular attractions, Victoria Park Zoo, which officials closed on account of the air raids.

1942

Commandos Rehearse

In the early weeks of March 1942, British commandos used Cardiff Docks to rehearse for one of the most successful but tragic raids of the Second World War. Many of those who trained at Cardiff were either among the 169 who died or the 216 taken prisoner after the attack on the dry dock at St Nazaire, in France. An ancient American destroyer, the *Campbeltown*, loaded with bombs and ammunition, was jammed into the lock gates and blown up. The action crippled the dry dock, one of only two in Europe which was big enough to serve the German battleship the *Tirpitz*, which was forced to stay in the Norwegian fjords before being sunk later in the war. The commander of the *Campbeltown*, Stephen Beattie, who was born in Montgomeryshire, was in a prisoner-of-war camp when it was announced that he had been awarded the Victoria Cross.

Two years later Cardiff Docks played another vital part in the war when a firm of engineers, headed by Jim Hennessy, made parts for the Mulberry Harbour which was used in the D-Day landings.

A merchant ship named SS *Cardiff* was sunk off Norway in 1942 – by a British submarine. At that time the *Cardiff* was sailing under the Nazi flag as it had been bought by the Germans in 1924. Llanrumney contractor Ray Chick discovered this in the 1990s after he bought a painting of a the first SS *Cardiff* for just £10. The vessel was built in 1875 and sank seven years later with the loss of all hands, including eight local men. With the help of Dr David Jenkins, of Cardiff Maritime Museum, Ray discovered that the ship, owned by Short and Dunne, of Cardiff, was carrying a cargo of coal when it floundered off the coast of Portugal on 23 October 1882. The SS *Cardiff* which was torpedoed in 1942 was built in 1888. Ray offered his £10 painting at an auction where it sold for £300.

HMS *Cardiff*, the ship that led the defeated German fleet into Scapa Flow in 1918 was officially adopted by the city in 1942, the year that the last barge operated on the Glamorgan Canal and when trolleybuses were first introduced to Cardiff. The Great Western Hotel, at the south end of St Mary Street, was taken over by the Red Cross to care for members of the armed services based in or travelling through Cardiff.

There was great joy when services were resumed at Llandaff Cathedral at Easter 1942 – some fifteen months after the historic building had been severely damaged by a German parachute mine which landed in the cemetery. Credit went to the army of volunteers who helped to clean up the mess caused by the explosion. There was one insight into human nature in the 1960s when one of the people involved in the work returned a valuable set of candlesticks which he had looted during the salvage operation.

1943

Dam Revenge

Chief Air Raid Warden Gilbert Shepherd looked around the war room at the City Hall, Cardiff, and told the exhausted men and women under his command that the latest raid which had brought death and destruction to the city, had been planned by a Nazi who knew Cardiff. That Nazi was almost certainly Hans Henri Künemann, who was managing director of the German-owned Flotmann Drill Factory in Allensbank Road, from 1935 until he fled Britain for Germany only twenty-four hours before war was declared on 3 September 1939. The factory was less than a mile away from the spot where the last parachute mines were dropped in the early hours of 18 May 1943, the last bombs to fall on Cardiff.

Künemann, who was born in Cologne in 1900, joined the Nazi Party in 1932 and his Nazi membership card was issued on 1 January 1933. It included the information that he was knowledgeable about Cardiff and Newport. Künemann's office was in Allensbank Road, the site of which was later occupied by a builders' yard until student flats were built there. Künemann used to take regular pleasure flights from Pengam Airport when he lived in Cardiff; excursions that enabled him to take arial photographs to assist the German Luftwaffe.

The raid in the early hours of 18 May was unexpected and vicious. It was the only time during the war that the Germans used their screaming Stuka bombers during a night raid on Britain. The siren sounded at 2.36 a.m. and the all-clear signal 83 minutes later. Sixty high explosives, parachute mines and hundreds of incendiary bombs were dropped on the city, killing 41 people, seriously wounding 52 and slightly injuring 76 others.

The worst incident was in St Agnes Road, at the Heath, where a row of modern houses received a direct hit, killing or burying a number of people. But there was one remarkable rescue operation. The home of the Pasley family in St Agnes Road was destroyed, but Mrs Ivy Pasley and her 2-year-old son Terry were found alive.

During the raid the rescue services saved 21 people and recovered 29 bodies from the rubble of their homes and shelters; a total of 4,300 houses and 140 shops were damaged. Bute Street station suffered considerable damage but the occupants of two nearby community shelters escaped with a few minor injuries. Two major fires broke out – at Brown Brothers, motorcycle dealers in Adam Street, and the Welsh Cold Stores in Pellet Street – and 45 minor fires were reported.

A number of bombs were dropped on the railway line between Queen Street Station and Cardiff General, and it was several days before a normal train service was possible. Premises on the docks were destroyed or damaged, and nearly all the telephone lines to the docks were put out of action. This seriously affected the Admiralty Offices at Jackson Hall in Westgate Street. The raid was the seventeenth and last on Cardiff Docks. The Guest Keen steelworks was hit for the first time during the war. It is believed it was spared earlier because had the Germans invaded Britain, they would have wanted to use the plant. Water was cut off from 441 houses, two churches and a nursing home, and supplies had to be provided by tankers.

The last two bombs, two parachute mines, fell at the junction of Maesycoed Road and Allensbank Road. The Germans were almost certainly targeting the American troops who were based at Heath Park or alternatively the Royal Ordnance Factory at Llanishen.

Künemann was not the only Nazi connected with Cardiff. Dr Friederick Schoberth, who was Professor of German at Cardiff University from 1928 to 1939, joined the Nazi Party in Berlin in 1942. He was on holiday in Germany when war broke out in September 1939 and joined the Nazi Party three years later. He was on the staff of the German Foreign Office and his jobs included editing the scripts of the hated broadcaster 'Lord Haw Haw', William Joyce, whose propaganda messages started with his infamous 'Jarmany Calling' introduction.

Before the war, American-born William Joyce, who held both British and Irish passports, lived in Colum Road, Cardiff, and also in Newland Street, Barry. He was captured trying to flee Germany in 1945 and was hanged for treason in London in 1946.

Dr Schoberth spent eighteen months in a prisoner-of-war camp before being released. He returned to Nuremberg where he helped to rebuild the city's university, which had been destroyed by Allied bombing. When John O'Sullivan, co-author of this book, asked Schoberth in 1986 if he had planned any of the raids on Cardiff, he replied: 'Cardiff, my lovely Cardiff. How could I? My daughter is buried in Llanishen churchyard.' Schoberth and his wife came back to Cardiff in the 1950s to visit the grave of their daughter, who died of meningitis at the age of 4 in 1937. Her headstone can be seen in the cemetery. Dr Schoberth did go to prison while in Cardiff – to entertain the inmates with German folk songs.

In July 1943 a German spy was arrested in Marlborough Road, Cardiff. He was a Czechoslovakian working at Cardiff Royal Infirmary and had been sending radio messages back to Germany. He almost certainly told his controller that Guy Gibson had led the 617 Squadron's Dambusters raid on Germany on 16/17 May 1943, and that is almost certainly the reason why the city was targeted on 18 May 1943. Gibson was married to Eve Moore, an actress who lived in Penarth, and the couple spent a lot of time in South Wales during the war. Gibson was in Penarth when the news came through that he had been awarded the Victoria Cross for his leadership of the Dambusters. Eight aircraft and fifty-three men were lost in the raid. Gibson died, at the age of twenty-six, in 1944 when his aircraft was shot down over Holland and he is buried in that country.

There was another possible reason for the city being targeted on the night of 18 May 1943. The area was not properly protected. Many of the gunners had left to take part in a competition at Aldershot with other ack-ack crews from various bases in the country. A report published in the *South Wales Echo* on 25 May 1943 said that the absence of ack-ack crews allowed the German aircraft to fly almost unopposed as they bombed Cardiff. As valid as this reason is for the last raid on the city, the Dambusters revenge raid was more likely to be the reason for Cardiff being targeted. Ack-ack crews from other parts of the country were taking part in the competition at Aldershot, so why didn't the Germans select other cities, some more strategically important than Cardiff?

❖   ❖   ❖

Cardiff-born 'Two-Ton' Tessie O'Shea was appearing at the city's New Theatre during the week of the last air raid and was staying in Plantagenet Street. She joined her neighbours in a communal shelter – and led a good old-fashioned singsong. 'We were scared, but there was a great spirit,' she said.

'Two-ton' Tessie O'Shea.

Tessie was not the only star to shine in Cardiff in 1943. Film star and comedian Bob Hope entertained American troops at the Cory Hall. He also topped the bill at the American Army Camp, at Cadoxton Moors, Barry, when one of his supporting artistes was Cardiff's own Stan Stennett. Bob Hope did not know at the time of his war visit to South Wales that his parents had lived in Greenwood Street, Barry, after being married in Cardiff. Bob visited Greenwood Street in the 1970s.

There was another important event in the entertainment field in Cardiff in 1943. A meeting was held at the Welsh Calvinistic Methodist Chapel in Crwys Road that led to the founding of the Welsh National Opera Company. Sian Hopkins, one of the city's many outstanding singers was born in 1943. It was also the year that the exiled King Haakon and Crown Prince Olaf of Norway visited Cardiff. The City Council's New Year gift to Cardiff was in the form of the Glamorgan Canal, which was bought for £44.

1944

Sporting Giant Killed

He played cricket for Glamorgan and England and rugby for Cardiff and Wales. He was capped as a goalkeeper for the Welsh hockey team and was also a British squash champion. He was Maurice Joseph Turnbull, a major in the Welsh Guards whose brilliant sporting career was ended by a sniper's bullet in Normandy on Friday 3 August 1944. He is buried in the war cemetery at Bayeux, the first town of importance to be liberated from the Germans after D-Day, 6 June 1944.

Maurice was one of six brothers who played rugby for Cardiff and in 1935 he followed his brother Bernard as scrum half for Wales. He made his debut for Glamorgan when he was only seventeen and still a schoolboy at Downside. He went on to captain Cambridge University and in 1930 was the first Glamorgan player to be selected for England in a test match in New Zealand. Maurice was secretary of Glamorgan Cricket Club but also found time to be sports editor of the *Welsh Catholic Times*, which was launched in Cardiff in 1931. Maurice married Elizabeth Brooke in Scunthorpe, Lincolnshire, on 8 September 1939, just five days after war was declared. The couple had met at the Cardiff Squash Club.

The Turnbull dynasty has played a prominent part in Cardiff life since they arrived from North Yorkshire in 1877 to expand the family shipping business. Harold Turnbull was Lord Mayor of Cardiff in the early 1920s and his son Gerald was Lord Mayor in 1973.

Flt Lt George Andrew Martin, of Colchester Avenue, Cardiff won the Distinguished Flying Cross for his bravery as a Spitfire pilot in the Balkan Air Force, founded by General Ike Eisenhower to attack the Germans in Yugoslavia. Martin got the title of Train Buster after destroying fifty-seven railway engines. He also shot down two German planes in dogfights and destroyed twelve more enemy planes on the ground. His aircraft was hit twenty times during the air battles.

The last air raid on Cardiff was on 18 May 1943, but on 27 March 1944, a man, his daughter and seven other women were killed in a friendly-fire incident while working at the ROF factory in Cardiff. The factory, where they were making parts for tanks, was hit by a shell fired at a lone German reconnaissance plane by an army gun crew at Gabalfa.

Although 75 per cent of the goods for American troops fighting in Europe was shipped through Cardiff Docks, the first signs that victory was in sight came when

Lt Gen D.G. Watson taking the salute as the Cardiff Home Guard paraded for the last time.

the Home Guard in Cardiff was disbanded, the ack-ack unit at Flat Holm, in the Bristol Channel, was stood down and blackout restrictions were lifted. The Freedom of Cardiff was given to the Welch Regiment, just four days after D-Day and a Merchant Navy Club was opened near Cardiff Central Station. The first prefab house was put on show in Wood Street, a type of dwelling that was needed to replace homes lost in the blitz. Former Lord Mayor George Williams gave the city 200 acres, which became Cefn-On Parc in a year when the South Wales Miners Federation was wound up. The first concert by the newly formed Welsh National Opera Company was held at the Empire Theatre on 23 April 1944. Although disbanded, former Home Guard members and other Civil Defence volunteers were back in action in November 1944 – helping flood victims in the Ely, Leckwith and Victoria Park areas.

Welshman Maj Tasker Watkins, VC, who, on 16 August 1944 at Barfour, Normandy, came under fire while advancing through booby-trapped corn fields. As the only remaining officer, Watkins led a bayonet charge with his remaining men against fifty enemy infantry, and practically obliterated them. He ordered his men to scatter and after charging and silencing an enemy machine-gun post, he returned them to safety. He not only saved his men, but single-handedly altered the course of the battle.

1945

The End of the War

Victory in Europe Day came on 8 May 1945, the day after the Germans had surrendered on all fronts. A BBC announcement was relayed by tannoy to the crowd gathered outside the City Hall at midnight. It was the signal for 50,000 men, women and children to cheer, dance and sing the night away in front of the floodlit hall. Blackout restrictions were still in force along the South Wales coast.

Cardiff rejoiced as lights went on again after six years of miserable blackout. The celebrations went on for days, with members of the armed services dancing and kissing factory and shop girls. There were similar scenes in most streets throughout the suburbs. Effigies of Hitler and other leading Nazis were hung from lamp-posts or burnt on bonfires. In a street off Broadway a piano was placed on the pavement and people gathered round a bonfire to sing 'Roll Out the Barrel' and 'Pack Up Your Troubles in Your Old Kit Bag – and Smile, Smile, Smile'. And how they smiled! The docks area was festooned with flags of many nations and Union Flags were painted in red, white and blue on communal shelters. Limbless troops from Rookwood Hospital hobbled down to the pubs in Llandaff City or gathered at the ancient Celtic cross outside the cathedral, still without a roof after a parachute mine landed in the graveyard in January 1941. Many people knelt in prayerful thanks or sang hymns with great gusto.

The next day magistrates granted thirty minutes extra drinking time for pubs and clubs, although Sir Lewis Lougher, JP, told Whitchurch Court that it should be a time for thanksgiving, not for boozing. He had little to worry about. Solicitor Charles Hallinan, representing the Licenced Victuallers' Association, forecast the pubs would run dry long before extra time. Services were held in churches and chapels of all denominations and mosques. Nowhere were the prayers more fervent than in the synagogues, as members of the Jewish community remembered the millions of their brethren who had been murdered by the Germans. Thousands attended an ecumenical service at the War

Order of service for the victory celebrations at Cathays Park, Cardiff, 1945.

Memorial in Cathays Park. The Lord Mayor took the salute at a victory parade and, echoing words spoken when the First World War ended, described the occasion as Cardiff's greatest moment. A fanfare of trumpets sounded across the city and hymns in Welsh and English were led by the Civil Defence Choir and local schoolchildren. Throughout the day, street parties were held, despite food still being on ration. One of the parties was in Montgomery Street, Roath, where the toast was FM Bernard Montgomery, their personal hero.

The celebrations were also tinged with sadness: hundreds of Cardiff people had died in action. The Memorial Book at the Seamen's Mission at Cardiff Bay catalogues the names of Merchant Navy men who died after sailing from their home port of Cardiff. A total of 355 Cardiff men, women and children were killed in air raids, and another 502 seriously injured. More than 10,000 Cardiff houses, shops, schools, churches and offices were either destroyed or severely damaged. Throughout Britain 26,920 men, 25,392 women and 7,736 children under the age of 16 were killed in the blitz. Another 86,175 people were gravely injured.

As Cardiff enjoyed the knees-up to celebrate VE Day there was still a dark cloud over the city. Many local men had been taken prisoners of war by the Japanese but their loved ones did not know whether they were alive or dead. Victory over Japan – VJ Day – came on 15 August 1945, after atomic bombs were dropped on Hiroshima and Nagasaki.

The survivors of the 77th Heavy Royal Artillery Regiment, which had been formed in Cardiff in 1939, were freed from Japanese prisoner-of-war camps on 11 September 1945 and arrived back in the city a month later. The 77th included many sportsmen, who spent the first three years of the war defending Cardiff from gun sites at Maerdy Farm in Rumney and Sloper Road, near Ninian Park. At weekends they entertained the public by playing soccer or rugby, cricket or hockey.

There were five members of the Cardiff City team in the 77th: Ernie Curtis, who had played in the 1927 FA cup winning team, Billy James, Bobby Tobin, Billy Baker and goalkeeper Jackie Pritchard. Billy James, who was born in Bridgend Street, Splott, scored the two goals that enabled Wales to draw with England at Ninian Park in the early 1940s. The rugby players included Wilf Wooler, who was also on the books of Barry Town football club and also an all-round cricketer who played for Glamorgan. Cardiff rugby players Les Spence and Fred Street were also in the battalion. In February 1942, the 77th was sent to Java and six weeks later were prisoners of war.

More than 300 men of the 77th died, many of them while working on the infamous Burma Railway. Cardiff's goalkeeper, Jackie Pritchard, died when a prison ship was sunk; his father lived at St Fagans, his wife at Fairwater. Maj Clive Mossford, of the Cardiff monumental sculpture firm, was officially reported as dead but arrived back in Cardiff three months after his regiment.

A captured German U-boat went on show in Cardiff in 1945.

One of the last battles of the Second World War was fought not in Germany but at Ninian Park Football Club. The weekend before VE Day, England beat Wales 3–2 in front of a 40,000 crowd. The *Echo*'s soccer pundit, 'The Citizen', described how Welsh fans had plastered the goalposts and field with leeks before jumping on the crossbars and behaving like monkeys. The police frog-marched some of the worst offenders from the field but one of the so-called hooligans hurled a photographer's box of films at one of the policemen.

The lads had no reason to behave like this as Cardiff City had given a trial to no fewer than 3,000 youngsters during the war years. A number of these were signed on by manager Cyril Spears.

1946

Love and War

American troops made both love and war in the 1940s, and in February 1946 the first group of twenty GI brides, some carrying children, gathered at Cardiff General Station to board a train for the first leg of their journey to America, aboard the *Queen Mary*. One of the brides was Avril Dexter, of Maitland Street, Cardiff. Her husband had served in the American Air Force and was waiting for her in Rochester, New York

State. Avril was seen off by her sister Hazel Wensley, also a GI bride, and her eight-month-old daughter, Caroline. They were to travel to America at a later date. At eighteen, Mary Ogden, of Wellington Street, Canton, Cardiff, was one of the youngest of the GI brides. Her new home would be in Pittsburgh, Pennsylvania.

As Cardiff continued to recover from the Second World War, a newcomer arrived who was going to make a big impact on the city for more than twenty years. The Revd Percy Brewster, an Elim Four Square Gospel preacher, attracted full houses at the City Temple in Cowbridge Road East. Up to a thousand singing, hand-clapping, enthusiastic worshippers of all ages attended his Sunday service, and at least 250 were there for his evening prayer meetings. Six hundred children attended the Sunday school.

The Revd Brewster, a preacher with a magnetic personality, was converted to the ministry after being a successful builder in the 1930s. Many who attended his

The Revd Percy Brewster, minister at the City Temple, Cardiff, who was famed for his magnetic personality.

services 'to be saved' were sick or disabled seeking comfort or possibly a cure from the pastor, who believed that prayer could help to heal the sick. This aspect of his ministry caused some controversy, and in 1961, when he was still a powerful figure in the city, the local hospital board were split over whether spiritual healers should be allowed to visit patients. They agreed by just seven votes to six to allow this, if the patient asked for it. And many of them did.

❖   ❖   ❖

Very few convicts have escaped while in the care of Cardiff Prison, but one man who succeeded was William 'Foxy' Fowler, who went on the run for five days after fleeing from a Cardiff Prison working party in Vale of Glamorgan in 1946.

It was the first of eight escapes from British prisons for the Barry-born offender, who boasted that no jail could hold him. There were breaks from Dartmoor, Devon, and Parkhurst on the Isle of Wight. That last break, in February 1961, nearly ended in farce. He reached the mainland by boat and persuaded a security guard at Porton Down germ warfare base to let him telephone for a taxi. The guard made him a cup of

Recaptured: William John Henry 'Foxy' Fowler, both wrists handcuffed, is flanked by two policemen after his 33-day freedom-run from Dartmoor in 1957. Just one of his many escapes.

tea while he was waiting. As the cab was driving away, the guard stopped it and asked the escaping prisoner to sign the visitor's book. He signed it 'Foxy Fowler, Parkhurst', and although his photograph and name had been splashed over newspapers the guard did not realise until his relief spotted Foxy's name when he came on duty.

Back in Cardiff valuable coal and shipping records were lost when a fire destroyed Merthyr House, in Stuart Street; the Welsh National Opera Company staged its first production at the Prince of Wales Theatre, in St Mary Street, and the frigate HMS *Llandaff* went to the breakers' yard.

1947

Bute of a Gift

In the tradition of his generous family, in 1947 the 5th Marquess of Bute endowed Cardiff with the greatest gift in its long history. He placed Cardiff Castle and 400 acres of the Castle grounds in the trust of the City Council. Only 12 acres of the site,

The 5th Marquess of Bute, John Crichton-Stuart, receives a casket containing a scroll from the Lord Mayor bearing the City Council's message of thanks for his magnificent gift to the city – Cardiff Castle, 11 September 1947.

A summer's day at Roath Park in 1947; the Scott Memorial Clock is in the background.

the land behind the animal wall, was excluded from the bequest. This site was donated to the Catholic Church, for the site of a new cathedral – a cathedral that is never likely to be built, although two priests, Fr John Lloyd and Fr Phillip Evans, had been imprisoned in the dungeons of the Castle before being hanged, drawn and quartered at Hangman's Hill, later developed as Crwys Road. The priests were named saints in the 1970s.

During the nineteenth century the 2nd and 3rd Marquess had developed Cardiff into a major port, exporting coal from their pits in the valleys. It was the 3rd Marquess, the richest man in the world, who engaged the architect William Burgess to transform the redundant castle into a home for himself and his family.

The first major development at the Castle after it was acquired by the Council was the establishment of the Welsh College of Music and Drama, which later moved to North Road. In the 1950s the Castle became a major tourist attraction and later hosted spectacular military tattoos. It was at the Castle in 1982 that Pope John Paul II and in 1998 Nelson Mandela were made Freemen of Cardiff.

In 1997 Cardiff Council made a successful application to the Heritage Lottery Fund for further development and conservation of the Castle. Work will continue over the next five years when further preservation of the keep will be done as well as restoration of the lavishly decorated Burges Apartments.

The Cardiff Rotary Club, founded in 1917, erected a plaque at Lavernock Point to mark the fiftieth anniversary of the first radio signal to be sent over water. The experiment that was to revolutionise communications was carried out by Guglielmo Marconi, with the help of an often forgotten engineer George Kemp. The message was sent from Flat Holm to Lavernock. The first words uttered were: 'Are you ready?'

The big freeze brought Cardiff virtually to a halt for seven weeks from 19 January 1947, making life a total misery for people struggling to recover from the war and coping with meagre rations of food.

1948

Biggest Funeral

What may have been the biggest funeral service ever held took place in Cardiff in 1948, when the bodies of 4,348 American servicemen who had died in action in Europe during the Second World War were loaded on the US *Lawrence Victor* at Cardiff Docks. Their remains were taken back to their home country after an emotional service on the foredeck of the ship, watched by thousands of people at the quayside. British and American troops formed the guard of honour, and military bands played as the bodies were loaded on the ship. It was one of the proudest but saddest days in the history of Cardiff.

A future Queen of England and a former Prime Minister were honoured in Cardiff in a year when a future President of the United States made a low-key visit to the city. Princess Elizabeth became the first woman Freeman of Cardiff, and Winston Churchill was also made a Freeman. Pomp and ceremony surrounded these events, but not so much notice was taken of the visit of film star Ronald Reagan to the Odeon Theatre, in Queen Street, to attend the showing of his film *The Voice of the Turtle*. Reagan was accompanied by film star Patricia Neil, who was presented with flowers by usherette Mrs D. Fowler. Reagan moved from films to politics and became President of the United States from 1981 to 1988. Other visitors to Cardiff around the time of Reagan's visit were the Kings of Comedy, Laurel and Hardy, who performed at the Philharmonic in St Mary Street.

Cricket fans had good reason to celebrate in 1948 when Glamorgan won the county championship for the first time; the team played most of its home games at the Cardiff Arms Park. The captain of the champion team was Johnny Clay, known throughout the sporting world as J.C. Clay, one of the founders of Glamorgan cricket who played

J.C. Clay, captain of Glamorgan's county championship-winning team.

for the county for twenty-eight seasons. During this time, he bagged a total of 1,317 first-class wickets with his slow left-hand spinners.

There were more celebrations when Wales beat England in the first postwar baseball international at Blackweir, Cardiff.

Cardiff poet Dannie Abse was still a medical student when his first volume of poetry *After Every Green Thing* was published in 1948. He went on to qualify as a doctor, specialising in chest diseases, and also published twelve volumes of poetry, two plays and two novels. Politics, especially in relation to his Jewishness and the nightmare of the Holocaust, was a prominent feature of his poetry. He was on record as saying that Auschwitz, where more than a million people were gassed by the Nazis, made him more of a Jew than Moses did.

Dannie was born in Cardiff on 22 September 1923. His older brothers were Wilfred, a psychologist, and Leo, a solicitor who became Labour MP for Pontypool. Leo's private member's bill made homosexuality legal in England and Wales. He also helped to draft an important bill dealing with divorce.

The Welsh Folk Museum opened at St Fagans in 1948, the year that scheduled flights restarted from Pengam Airport, Cardiff. The Hayes Island snack bar opened in a building used as a parcel depot in the days of the trams, and Michael Barratt, who as Shakin' Stevens made the pop charts, was born in Ely.

1949

Outstanding Bravery

The 14th Cardiff (Lord Mayor's Own) Scout Group was involved in a tragic incident along the South Wales coast on 28 May 1949. One of its members drowned in attempting to save friends who were swept away as they tried to cross from Sully Island

The causeway between Swanbridge and Sully Island.

to Swanbridge beach. Scout John Davies, aged 12, of Connaught Road, reached safety, and although not a strong swimmer went back into the sea to help two of his friends. He was swept away and drowned but was posthumously awarded the Albert Medal and the Scouts' Bronze Cross, the organisation's highest honour for gallantry.

Fourteen-year-old Margaret Vaughan, of Whitchurch, risked her own life to bring two of the struggling scouts to safety. The Scouts were swept from the causeway between the island and the beach by the rip of the tide, which at that point is the one of the highest in the world, second only to Fundy Bay in Nova Scotia.

Margaret, who was enjoying a day out at Swanbridge, ran over the rocky foreshore into the sea and battled against the fast-flowing tide and currents to bring the two scouts to safety. She, too, was awarded the Albert Medal, later upgraded to the George Cross – the youngest female ever to win the highest honour for civilians. Rover Scout James Anthony Rees was awarded the Scouts' Bronze Cross for his part in the rescue. A third scout, 11-year-old Michael Gleeson, of Heathwood Road, was saved by Richard George, of Sully, who with the help of another man rowed to the rescue.

The day after the incident, Margaret was back in the water – representing Penarth Grammar School in a gala at the local baths. As a schoolgirl, Margaret had acted as one of the pacemakers for Bristol Channel swimmers, including Jenny James, of Pontypridd who also conquered the English Channel. Later in 1949 Jenny swam from Swanbridge to Weston-super-Mare, an estimated 17 miles, in 10 hours 5 minutes.

Scout John Davies has not been forgotten. His grave is included on the Heritage Trail at Cathays Cemetery. The headstone, which features the Scouts' Emblem, was paid for with a £100 grant from the Carnargie Trust. The Trust also paid for a silver cup, which Monkton House, John's School, awarded annually to the pupil making the most progress in swimming.

❖   ❖   ❖

The great diversity of Cardiff's population was illustrated in 1949 when the first British Muslim conference was held in the city and the Bryn Taf, the first Welsh-language primary school, opened. This was also the year when the Welsh College of Music and Drama was accommodated in Cardiff Castle and Churchill Way, then the city's widest road, opened. The old Glamorgan Canal feeder runs underneath the dual carriageway road named after Winston Churchill.

❖   ❖   ❖

Sir Robert Hughes, who was Lord Mayor in 1905, died in April 1949, the year that some of the best-known and successful people were born: Ken Follett (right), who was a reporter with the *South Wales Echo* before becoming a multimillionaire novelist; footballer and Welsh team manager John Toshack; rugby star J.P.R. Williams; actress Angharad Rees and folk singer Heather Jones.

1950

Jenny's Big Splash

The Guildford Crescent Baths, which stood on the corner of Churchill Way until they were demolished, were divided into three 25-yard sections: one for men, one for women and one which could be used by both sexes. Paulo Radmilovic, who won four Olympic gold medals, trained there, and so did Jenny James, the greatest long-distance swimmer produced by Wales. Pontypridd-born Jenny was a member of Cardiff Ladies Swimming Club in July 1950, when she became the first woman to swim the Bristol Channel in both directions. At the age of 20 she completed the 17-mile leg from Swanbridge to Weston-super-Mare in a time of 10 hours 5 minutes in September 1949: ten months later she swam from Weston-super-Mare to Penarth in 8 hours 29 minutes. Jenny used to joke that she had to swim home because she couldn't afford the fare! In 1951 she became the first Welsh-born swimmer to master the English Channel, from France to Dover in 13 hours 55 minutes. By this time she had turned professional and won £250 for finishing eleventh. She took part in many other long-distance swims and was the first

Jenny James poses for a photograph just before she began her attempt to swim from Ilfracombe to Lundy Island – a distance of 17 miles.

Welsh person to swim the length of Lake Windermere. Jenny gave up long-distance swimming in the 1960s and became a coach.

The Marquess of Bute followed up his generous gift of Cardiff Castle to the city by presenting Castell Coch, the Red Castle, at Tongwynlais (left), to the care of the Ministry of Works and later Cadw. The castle attracts visitors from near and far. It was also the setting of the film *The Black Prince*.

Trams ran in Cardiff until 1950.

This was the year that the last tram ran from St Mary Street to Whitchurch Road and when the world's first scheduled helicopter service, between Cardiff and Liverpool, was inaugurated. It was the year that speedway racing was resumed at Penarth Road; the College of Art, in The Friary, and the teachers training college were both opened; the last shipment of coal left Bute Dock and the Labour Exchange opened in Westgate Street (it was later demolished to make way for the Millennium Stadium). Two sporting giants were born in Cardiff this year: Terry Yorath, who played soccer for Wales and also managed the national team, and Martyn Woodroffe, who won many honours at swimming.

1951

Prayer and Music

Within weeks the deaths took place of two men whose lives had had a great impact on Wales, Cardiff and the world. Evangelist Evan Roberts died in a home for elderly people in Penylan, Cardiff, on 29 January 1951 and composer, singer and film star Ivor Novello died on 6 March.

Evan Roberts was a Carmarthenshire Welsh Calvinistic Methodist preacher who launched and led the Welsh Revival that packed chapels throughout Wales in

1904–5. His brand of Christianity spread throughout the world, especially in America where its spirit lives on into the twenty-first century. After bowing out of public life, Roberts became a recluse and lived in various places, including Brighton and Leicester, before residing in Rhiwbina, Cardiff. He was 72 when he died, regretting that he had never married. He is buried behind Moriah Chapel at Loughor. Carmarthenshire, close to where he sparked off the greatest religious revival Wales has ever seen.

The death of Ivor Novello at the age of 58 marked the end of a brilliant and glamorous career that made him the toast, not only of the West End, but of the

troops who fought and died in the trenches during the First World War. His nostalgic song 'Keep The Home Fires Burning' was said to have been worth a battalion of men in the fight against the Germans. Between the wars Novello (left) starred in the London West End shows for which he wrote the music. The most acclaimed of these was the 1939 hit *The Dancing Years*. He also went to Hollywood and appeared in films, but the stage remained his first love. He wrote his musicals in the style of operettas and was one of the last major composers of this form.

Ivor was born in a house called Llwyn-yr-Eos ('Grove of Nightingales'), in Cowbridge Road East, on 15 January 1893; a memorial plaque was placed on the house in the early 1980s. His love for music was influenced by his mother, Dame Clara Novello Davies (1861–1943), a noted singer and teacher. Her husband, David, was a tax collector.

The composer, who was idolised by First World War troops, was jailed for a short while during the Second World War for a black market petrol offence. The shame of this broke his spirit, but he continued to appear on stage until the day before his sudden death in 1951. Novello risked being sent to jail for another reason, he was a homosexual in an age when it was considered a major crime. For thirty-five years, he was the lover of the British actor Bobby Andrews, and he also had an affair with the British poet and writer Siegfried Sassoon.

In the twenty-first century the record industry keeps the Novello musical fires burning at the annual ceremonies in which song writers and arrangers, rather than the performing artistes, are honoured with Ivor Novello Awards.

Another great character, Alderman R.G. Hill-Snook died at the age of ninety-two at his home in Ty-Gwyn, Penylan, Cardiff, in January 1951. He served on the City Council for thirty-six years, from 1918 to 1954. When he was Lord Mayor in 1930 he donated 28 acres of land at the Wenallt to the city. His parents had come to Cardiff from Shepton Mallet in Somerset in 1850, when Hill-Snook was only one year old. The family had bread and cake shops in City Road and Clifton Street but R.G. Hill-Snook was known as the man who wore a top hat and a buttonhole.

Millions of Jews died in concentration camps during the Second World War, and the Cardiff Jewish community also made sacrifices with at least twenty-five of its members being killed in action. A memorial to these men was unveiled at the Cathedral Road synagogue in 1951, when the order of service included a photograph and pen picture of each of the victims. It is a unique document as most war memorials carry only the names of those who died and not where or how they died. The Cardiff Jewish Ex-Servicemen's Association has a copy of the document.

Baseball, the game the Welsh taught the Americans, was enjoying a golden era. Freddy Fish (right) once hit nine successive fours standing as last man, wearing the black-and-white striped shirt of Grange Albion – a world record at any standard. He hit the ball hard enough for a tenth four, but collapsed running between the second and third pegs. Tommy 'Cock Robin' Denning, who had intense pride in his own ability, gained twelve caps for Wales at baseball.

Albert Stitfall, whose brother Ron played fullback for Cardiff City, struck fifty-six in a single innings for Splott US against Penylan in 1951. A few years later Paddy Hennessy bowled his way into the record books when playing for Wales at Maindy Stadium – he dismissed England in their first innings for just six runs.

The tollgate on Penarth Road closed in 1951, much to the delight of drivers who had to pay on their way to and from Cardiff. This was also the year that the Glamorgan Canal was finally closed and when speedway racing started a short life at Penarth Road Stadium. Sophia Gardens Pavilion, built to mark the Festival of Britain, opened in April, and Maindy Stadium opened the following month. Edith Richardson became the first woman police inspector in Cardiff, and the old drawbridge at Cardiff Castle was replaced by a permanent structure.

1952

Wrong Man Hanged

The last man to be hanged in Cardiff was a Somali seaman Mahmood Mattan, who was wrongly found guilty of murdering shopkeeper Lily Volpert in Bute Street in 1952. Forty-five years later the man who was cruelly described by his defence counsel as a 'half savage beast of nature', was granted a posthumous pardon by three Appeal Court judges in London. 'My husband can now rest in peace,' said his widow Laura, who had campaigned for decades to prove his innocence.

Her first success came when she got permission to remove her executed husband's body from Cardiff Prison and rebury it in Western Cemetery, less than a mile from her home. Then, with the backing and legal skills of Cardiff solicitor Bernard de Maid she succeeded in getting the case reviewed in the Appeal Court. The judges totally discredited the evidence of Harold Cover, the key witness in the murder trial. He was in the Appeal Court but not called to give evidence and in 1969 Cover himself was jailed for eighteen years for attempting to murder his own daughter. Another Somali, Tahir Gass, who was seen near Lily Volpert's shop on the night of her murder, was sent to Broadmoor Asylum in 1954 after being found guilty of another murder.

John O'Sullivan, the co-author of this book, claimed in 1969 that the wrong man had been hanged for the Volpert murder. He had a front-page lead in a Sunday newspaper for four successive weeks and also had questions asked in the House of Commons, but to no avail. It was another twenty-nine years before justice was done.

The scene outside the City Hall when the Lord Mayor, Alderman W. Muston, read the proclamation of the Coronation in 1952.

This was the year that the Empire House telephone exchange opened in Park Street; it was later demolished to make way for the Millennium Stadium. One of the porches of the telephone exchange was home for many years to a man of the street, a Lithuanian named John. He slept there standing up each night, and the shape of his body could be clearly seen on the wall. He later went to the Cyrenian Hostel in Tresillian Terrace, one of a number of hostels for the homeless in Cardiff.

In the field of entertainment, Cardiff, despite strong opposition from Church leaders, voted in a referendum in favour of cinemas opening on Sundays. The first Sunday films were shown the following March but surprisingly there were not many full houses.

The BBC television transmitter started operating at Wenvoe, and the Welsh National Opera Company appeared at Sophia Gardens Pavilion with a production of *Nabucco*. The Prudential Buildings, which housed the Inland Revenue and later became the Hilton Hotel, opened in Kingsway; Gus Risman, at the age of 41, became the oldest man to play in a Rugby League cup final and sculptor Sir William Goscombe John died on 5 December.

1953

Angel of the Blind

The Institute for the Blind workshops and headquarters on Newport Road, Cardiff, was opened by Sir Walter Monkton in 1953, two years after the foundation stone had been laid by the Duchess of Gloucester. The building was named after Frances Batty Shand, whose pioneering work for the blind and visually impaired dated back to 1865. The daughter of a Jamaican plantation owner, she moved to Cardiff with her brother on the death of her father. At first she was concerned with the ragged Irish children in Cardiff, then she met Frederick Hallet, a representative of the Blind Bible Society, who told her of the plight of the many blind men in Cardiff. Miss Shand opened a small workshop in the Canton area of Cardiff, employing four blind men making baskets for the coal ships sailing from Cardiff.

Within a year, larger premises were purchased at Byron Street in the Roath area and ten men were employed. In 1868 a third move was made to Longcross Street, off Newport Road, within 300 yards of Shand House. Miss Shand died in Switzerland in 1885, and her body was brought back to Cardiff for burial. Her grave is on the heritage trail at Cathays Cemetery. The Longcross premises she founded were destroyed during a German air raid in the 1940s.

The death took place in 1953 of Henry Vaughan Lanchester, the architect who designed Cardiff City Hall and Law Courts, acclaimed as some of the finest civic buildings in the world. Dr Lanchester, a pioneer in town planning, died at the age of 89, at his home at Seaford, Sussex, forty-seven years after his masterpieces were completed. Lanchester, who gained the Royal Gold Medal for Architecture in 1934, also designed the Central Hall at Westminster, Deptford Town Hall, and Birmingham Hospital.

This was the year that the first scheduled flights were introduced between Cardiff and Paris. The Royal Welsh Show was held in Cardiff for the last time and the premiere of Arwel Hughes's opera *Menna* was held at Sophia Gardens Pavilion. Thornhill Crematorium was opened and the open-air market moved from Hayes Island to Mill Lane. Speedway racing ended at Penarth Road.

1954

Miners Walk with Pride

Without coal exports, Cardiff may have remained a small fishing port and may never have graduated to a city and become capital of Wales. The link between the black diamonds and the city was firmly sealed in 1954, when the first of many Miners Galas was held in Cardiff. Miners and their families from all over South Wales walked to the stirring music of brass bands through the crowded streets of Cardiff, with banners flying. Leading the processions were miners' leaders such as Will Paynter, Dai 'keep your powder dry' Francis, Will Whitehead and Glyn Williams and, during the year-long strike in the 1980s, Arthur Scargill. Leo Abse, known for his elegant Edwardian-style dress, donned a cloth cap to walk with the miners, who had no problem getting the support of other Labour MPs. There were over a hundred pits in Wales in the 1950s, but after the Thatcher government wielded its axe in the 1980s, there was only one deep pit left – Tower Colliery, Hirwaun, bought out by the local miners led by Tyrone O'Sullivan, whose father had been killed in an accident in the pit. In 1995, at the instigation of Lord Mayor Rickie Ormonde, the miners were given the Freedom of Cardiff, the city they helped to build with their sweat, guts, blood, lungs, tears and many lives.

Your starter for ten: what do a sculpture at Llandaff Cathedral and the writer Oscar Wilde have in common? The answer is Sir Jacob Epstein, who designed Wilde's tomb in the Cemetery of Père Lachaise, Paris, following the author's death in 1912. Forty-two years later Epstein created the magnificent but controversial *Christ in Majesty*, which now dominates the inside of the twelfth-century cathedral. The building was built by the Normans in 1107, close to a site associated with the Celtic saints Dyfrig and Teilo. Many extensions and alterations have been made to the cathedral, which celebrates its 900th anniversary in 2007. Cromwell's men once used it as an ale house, but it was the German Luftwaffe which did the most damage when they dropped a parachute mine on it during the blitz in 1941. Extensive damage was done to both the roof and the inside of the cathedral, and because of building restrictions it was another thirteen years before the historic landmark was restored, not only to its former glory but also modernised, under the guidance of architect George Pace. His challenge was to make the cathedral more spacious and fit for the twentieth century without destroying the ancient features. He reinforced the concrete arch between the nave and the choir, and it is there that Epstein's aluminium stands.

The cathedral's features also include the Welch Regiment Memorial Chapel and also the Lady Chapel, on which are carved many flowers, such as the marigold, whose names are associated with the Mother of Christ. There are justifiable claims that, because of its cathedral, Llandaff was a city long before the title was given to Cardiff. Llandaff and the suburb of Llanishen did not officially come into the Cardiff boundaries until 1922.

Bart Wilson, the father of the Bluebirds, died in Canton, at the age of eighty-four on 19 November 1954, some sixty-six years after he expanded the Riverside cricket team to embrace the game of soccer. From that humble start in 1899, Riverside Football Club, which played in the Cardiff and District League, developed into Cardiff City Football Club, which joined the Football League in 1920, were beaten finalists in the FA Cup at Wembley in 1925, beat Arsenal 1–0 to win the FA Cup in 1927, won promotion from various leagues on ten occasions and were winners of the Welsh Cup numerous times. For more than four decades Wilson's grave at Western Cemetery remained unmarked, but this was remedied in 1999 when Cardiff City Football Club arranged for a headstone to be placed there, a fitting tribute a hundred years after the Riverside Club was formed.

This was the year that the Duke of Edinburgh was given the Freedom of the City, Cardiff Airport was transferred from Pengam to Rhoose and the new central bus station opened. Llandaff Technical College opened in Western Avenue, and the old Technical College in Dumfries Place became the headquarters of the Students Union, which was later transferred to Park Place. Sloper Road Stadium closed, the *Empire News*, the first Sunday newspaper in Wales, was launched and the Welsh National Opera Company staged its first production at the New Theatre, which became its main venue over the next forty years.

1955

Capital of Wales

When Cardiff was made a city on 28 November 1905, the process involved a Royal Charter signed personally by King Edward VII. The lengthy document, written in language that only the best legal brains could attempt to understand, upgraded the former Borough of Cardiff to a city, with the right to elect a Lord Mayor.

When the city was named as capital of Wales on 20 December 1955, the honour was bestowed in just fifty-nine words uttered by a government minister in the House of Commons when he was asked by David Llewellyn, MP for his view on the lobbying of the Association of Welsh Local Authorities. No Royal Charter, no royal signature, no wordy unintelligible document, just fifty-nine words in an answer to a question put to the Secretary of State for the Home Department and Minister for Welsh Affairs. The reply given to the House was: 'The government have been impressed by the volume of support in Wales that Cardiff is a city which should most appropriately be regarded as the capital of Wales, and in deference to this view the government is prepared to recognise Cardiff as the capital of the Principality. No formal measures are necessary to give effect to this decision.' The words that made Cardiff the youngest capital city in Europe were spoken by Major Gwilym Lloyd George, MP, the son of former Prime Minister David Lloyd George, who was made a Freeman of Cardiff in 1911.

After the official announcement in the Commons, Gwilym Lloyd George described it as a moment of deep emotion for the people of Wales and said the decision was the fruit of thirty years of inspiration and endeavour.

Cardiff was determined to make up for the lack of official pomp and ceremony when the historic decision was proclaimed from the City Hall. The Lord Mayor had an escort of soldiers from the Welch Regiment when he addressed a small crowd outside the City Hall. The Council then travelled to the Coal Exchange in Cardiff Dockland where the proclamation was made to assembled businessmen and traders who loudly cheered the news. It was the best Christmas present that Cardiff could have been given. Major Gwilym Lloyd George, the Home Secretary who made the capital announcement, was rewarded for his decision when he was made a Freeman of Cardiff in 1956.

Sadly, as Cardiff was made a capital, the death took place of Percy Bush, one of the heroes of the Welsh rugby victory over New Zealand in 1905, the year the old borough gained city status. Percy was an outstanding fly-half but was also remembered for an incident when Cardiff played the All Blacks in 1905. As the All Blacks performed their traditional haka war dance before the kick-off, Percy ran to the touchline, picked up a spear and shield and ran yelling at the New Zealanders. In 2005 Wales adopted their own form of haka – thousands of fans singing the stirring hymn 'Bread of Heaven'.

The Lord Mayor of Cardiff announced the news in 1955 that the city had been made capital of Wales.

The same year that Cardiff was made a capital city, a new synagogue opened at Penylan, the Queens Cinema in Queen Street closed its doors for the last time, the University College playing fields were established in Llanrumney and the frigate HMS *Llandaff* was launched.

1956

Death of a Marquess

John Crichton-Stuart, the 5th Marquess of Bute, who gifted the Castle to Cardiff in 1947, died on 15 August 1956. He was succeeded to the title by his eldest son, Sir John Crichton-Stuart. The 5th Marquess was a keen ornithologist and served in the Royal Navy during the Second World War.

Cardiff was not only the greatest coal-exporting port in the world, for seventy years it was a fishing port, the home of the Neale and West trawler fleet. But the fishing industry ended in Cardiff in 1956, forty years after the local trawlers had helped in the Atlantic battle against German U-boats. The trawlers were armed with 3lb or 12lb guns, just in case the Germans abandoned their code of not attacking fishing boats.

A long left from Joe Erskine is blocked by Johnny Williams during their bout on 26 August 1956.

Joe Erskine, a gentle giant who did his native Cardiff proud, won the vacant British heavyweight title by beating Johnny Williams on points in August 1956. He went on to win the Empire title by beating the great Henry Cooper on points over fifteen rounds in 1957. But Cooper, who once floored Muhammad Ali (Cassius Clay), had his revenge against Joe by knocking him out in their next three meetings. Joe quit the ring in 1964, at the age of thirty. He died in Cardiff in 1990, and one of the pall-bearers at his funeral was his greatest rival, Henry Cooper.

Velindre Hospital, which has been in the front line of the treatment and fight against cancer in Cardiff, was opened by Princess Margaret in 1956, the year that the Welch Regiment Memorial was dedicated at Llandaff Cathedral, and the year that the Bath and West Show was held in Cardiff for the last time.

1957

Our Shirl

It was a song that could have been written as an anthem for the port of Barry, but in 1957 it provided the launching pad for the career of Cardiff's most famous daughter, Shirley Bassey, who was born in Bute Street on 8 January 1937. She made the Top Ten with 'The Banana Boat Song' around the time that Barry secured the port-saving contract to handle the Geest Banana boats from the Caribbean.

Shirley was the seventh child of Henry, a Nigerian seaman, and Eliza, who was from the north of England. The girl from Tiger Bay was living in Tremorfa when she left school at the age of fifteen in 1952. She worked in a local factory and sang in local clubs where she was discovered by bandleader Jack Hylton, who persuaded her to go to London in 1955.

While still a teenager, she made the charts with 'Kiss Me, Honey Honey, Kiss Me' and her first Number One, 'As I Love You'. In 1959 she won many more fans, both in America and Britain, with 'As Long As He Needs Me', from the musical *Oliver!* She was a well-established cabaret star when she rocked the music world with 'Goldfinger', the first of three theme songs she sang for James Bond films. The others are 'Diamonds Are for Ever' and 'Moonraker'.

In the 1960s, when her popularity matched that of the Beatles, she had further hits, including 'I Who Have Nothing', 'Big Spender' and 'No Regrets'. Shirley's star shone throughout the '70s but virtually disappeared in the '80s. There was always a full house when she sang in Cardiff, and there was great rejoicing in the city when, in 1997, as she reached 60, she teamed up with Bath's Propellerheads, a move that introduced her to a new generation of dance fans.

When she wore a Welsh Dragon dress and sang at the opening ceremony for the World Rugby Cup at the Millennium Stadium in Cardiff, she was rewarded with an ovation that was the envy of the great sportsmen who have appeared there. Shirley also topped the bill at the concert to mark the launch of the Wales National Assembly, less than a mile away from where she was born, and she was one of the stars at the opening of the Cardiff Millennium Centre in 2004. By this time she was Dame Shirley Bassey, having been included in the honours list in 2002. But to the people of Cardiff she will always be 'Our Shirl', who as a schoolgirl had sung at the Rainbow Club in Bute Street.

Shirley Bassey was not the only singer from Tiger Bay who was making an impression in the entertainment world in 1957. Singing at the Pineapple Club in Butetown was Irene Spettie, who was earning £6 a week in a dress factory by day and topping this up by singing at night. Irene was spotted by local bandleader Waldini, who groomed her for stardom, and the *South Wales Echo* feature writer Gareth Bowen. They and the legendary Cardiff guitarist Vic Parker encouraged her to turn professional, and Irene headed for London where she changed her name to Lorne Lesley. In 1964 she made her debut at the London Palladium on a bill headed by Frankie Vaughan: a last-minute chance when Cilla Black was taken ill. Lorne's first professional engagement had been at the Victoria in Cowbridge Road and she 'died a death'. She was not with her people in Butetown but among strangers. She told Waldini that if she did a jive down Queen Street in a flared skirt people would consider her common. Butetown would have loved it. Once she had conquered her nerves and hit the London nightclub scene, Lorne became a star and more than thirty years later was still singing. The chances are that people are more likely to recognise not Lorne, but her husband in a crowd. He is antiques dealer David Dickinson, who features in many television shows. Older people still talk about Irene Spetti, the factory girl who some say was as good as Bassey.

Singer Lorne Lesley says goodbye to children living in her street before moving to London to appear at the leading Mayfair club, Churchill's.

The world press descended on St Joseph's Convent School, North Road, Cardiff, to find out as much as they could about a former pupil, Joan O'Callaghan, who, under the assumed name of Anna Kashfi, had married Hollywood superstar Marlon Brando in October 1957. On one occasion the headmistress, Mother Finbarr, chased a *Paris Match* photographer down the drive after he had tried to snap her ringing the school bell.

Brando met his future wife in 1955, when she had a small part in a Spencer Tracey film called *The Mountain*. She was born in India and convinced Brando she was an Indian Princess. In reality she was the daughter of a railway engineer and worked as a waitress after leaving school, living in Newfoundland Road, Cathays, before going to Hollywood. Brando was furious when he learnt the truth, and the couple separated in 1958 – the same year as their son Christian was born. In 1991 Christian was jailed for killing his stepsister's boyfriend. His mother, who still used the name Anna Kashfi, ended up living in a caravan in America.

❖   ❖   ❖

This was the year that saw the closure of the *Cardiff Times*, one of the greatest sources of Cardiff's history. The Welsh Guards were given the Freedom of the City, and Epstein's *Majesty of Christ* was consecrated at Llandaff Cathedral.

1958

Host to Empire

Cardiff had been a capital city for just three years when it hosted the greatest sporting event in its history, the 1958 Empire Games. Sportsmen and women from countries that made up the former British Empire descended on Cardiff to compete against each other in athletics, swimming, diving, boxing, rowing, cycling, bowls and fencing. To mark the occasion, Her Majesty The Queen handed over at Buckingham Palace a specially designed baton, containing a message from her to be carried by a relay of 664 runners to Cardiff. It was relayed at the opening ceremony at Cardiff Arms Park and read to the capacity crowd assembled in the stadium. It is now an integral part of the Commonwealth Games.

But let's go back to 1958 and the brilliant performance of Howard Winstone of Merthyr, who, as a bantamweight, won Wales' only gold medal at the Empire Games, by beating the Australian Oliver Frankie Taylor. Howard turned professional and became world champion when he beat Vicente Saldivar in 1965. Cardiff-born Malcolm Collins won a silver in the ring. Welsh boxers who won bronze medals at the Cardiff Games were light-heavyweight Robert Higgins and heavyweight Robert Please.

The only athlete to get a medal for Wales in 1958 was long-distance runner John Merriman, who came second to the outstanding Australian Dave Power, who also won the marathon at the Cardiff Games in 1958.

The Wales Empire Pool was built for the Empire Games in 1958 and demolished to make way for the Millennium Stadium.

Fencing is not a sport that hits the headlines in Wales, but in 1958, the Welsh foil team and the Welsh sabre team both won bronze medals. The toast of cycling fans was Welshman Don Skene, who won bronze in the 10-mile scratch road race. There was also bronze medal smiles on the faces of the Welsh coxless-four rowing team, David Edwards, John Fage, David Prichard and John Edwards.

The Wales Empire Pool was built in Wood Street for the 1958 Games, and the great Australian Dawn Frazer struck gold when she won the 110-yards freestyle. The Empire Pool was demolished in 1998 to allow development of the Millennium Stadium. There are hopes that a new Olympic-style pool will be included in the Sports Village planned for Cardiff Bay.

The Queen was not well enough to attend the closing ceremony of the 1958 Empire Games, but her recorded message broadcast at the Arms Park revealed her intention to make her 10-year-old son Charles the Prince of Wales when he came of age. It was a promised kept in 1969 when Prince Charles was officially given the title in a ceremony at Caernarfon Castle.

When the Queen's message rang out across the Arms Park in 1958 the crowd spontaneously sang 'God Bless the Prince of Wales', which was last heard to greet the previous holder of the title who went on to become King Edward VIII.

❖   ❖   ❖

Labour gained control of the City Council for the first time in 1958, the year that TWW launched the first commercial TV channel from a site at Pontcanna. The Glamorgan Canal in the centre of Cardiff was filled in; Princess Margaret officially opened the YWCA hostel in Newport Road and Llandaff Cathedral School moved to Cardiff Road. The Festival of Wales was launched with a 'Salute to the Capital' parade in May 1958, and the following month the first Llandaff Festival was held.

1959

Plane Crashes on City

It is every city's and town's nightmare – an aeroplane plunging out of the sky and crashing on or near a residential area. It was a nightmare that became a reality for Cardiff onto 6 May 1959. Four people were killed when the twin-engine Dove aircraft they were in crashed on North Road, close to Blackweir playing fields where 400 schoolboys were enjoying a sports day.

The aircraft, owned by Lec Refrigeration Company, of Bognor Regis, exploded as it hit a parked van. Fortunately nobody on the ground was killed, but the pilot and three passengers all died in the burning wreck. Firemen took thirty minutes to control the fierce fire and then recovered the bodies from the wreckage. There were charred propellers and wheels, the ragged edge of a wing, clothing intermingled with parts of the plane and what remained of two bicycles that had been standing against a wall.

Dorothy Elias, of Maindy Road, had just got off a number 38 bus when she saw the plane crash. As people started running towards it she screamed at them to stay back and seconds later the petrol tanks exploded. Thirteen-year-old Derek Edwards, of Ty Mawr Road, Rumney, who was taking part in the sports, said the aeroplane circled the area three times and the pilot signalled that he was attempting to land on the playing fields. The crowd scattered but the plane overshot the field and crashed near a garage on North Road. Builder George Foreman was working only eight yards away as the plane skimmed over the chimney tops before crashing. He and the dozen men working in the yard of Miles Brothers building contractors jumped over the wall like frightened rabbits. They warned people to get out of the way as flaming petrol ran along the pavement and into the drains.

The plane had taken off from Sophia Gardens, where the Ideal Homes Exhibition was being held. Among those who turned down the chance of a flight were the Chief Constable of Cardiff and *South Wales Echo* reporter Sonia Davies, who returned to

Thomson House 'flaming mad' because the deputy news editor, Jack Parker, had told her she couldn't fly because she was not insured for the trip. She didn't know the plane had crashed until she arrived at the office.

❖   ❖   ❖

Cardiff's first woman Lord Mayor, Alderman Mrs Helena Evans, after her investiture ceremony on 26 May 1959.

Alderman Helena Evans was elected the first woman Lord Mayor of Cardiff in 1959, the year that St David's Cathedral reopened, eighteen years after being destroyed in the blitz of March 1941, and the year that the last service was held at the Norwegian church on its original site at Cardiff Docks. It was later demolished and rebuilt as part of Cardiff Bay. The last passing-out parade of Welch Regiment recruits took place at Maindy Barracks, before the headquarters were transferred to Crickhowell. The College of Domestic Art and Waterhall School, The Urdd (Welsh League of Youth) opened, in Conway Road. Manor Way opened in Whitchurch; the Canadian Roy Thomson bought the *Western Mail and Echo* from the Kemsley family and the first Welsh Games were held at Maindy Stadium and the Empire Pool. Another memorable event was the première at the Gaumont Cinema of the film *Tiger Bay* starring John Mills and his daughter Hayley.

1960

Historic Landmarks

Plans were being made in 1960 to demolish two of Cardiff's best-known Nonconformist landmarks, Wood Street Congregational Church in Wood Street and Bethany Baptist Chapel, in St Mary Street. The Wood Street church – on the site where Southgate House now stands – was once the home of a circus, and the star performer was Blondin, a tightrope walker. More than 2,000 people gathered at the chapel before it was demolished for a service conducted by the American Evangelist Billy Graham by radio link. The building was originally erected in the mid-nineteenth century as a Temperance Hall. A warren of working-class houses was built around the hall, and the area became known as Temperance Town until it was bulldozed in 1937.

As the campaign for temperance faded, the hall was acquired by Ginnett's Circus. The Revd William Watkiss, a former miner from Staffordshire and a noted preacher and evangelist, started to hold services there in 1868. He served the church until his death in January 1882. In 1807 the Baptists acquired an old stable in St Mary Street for £306 and this was eventually developed into Bethany Baptist Chapel, which was nearly 160 years old when it was demolished. The site is remembered for another reason. A member of the congregation, a Brother Hopkins, buried his dead child in a corner of the old stable garden. It caused a sensation as it was the first Dissenting burial ground in Cardiff.

The *Western Mail and Echo*, Cardiff's main newspaper, moved offices from 102–4 St Mary Street, on the corner of Golate, to Thomson House in Havelock Street on 28 November 1960. The *Western Mail*, which had been launched by the 3rd Marquess of Bute in 1869, was originally published at the old hostelry, the Cornish Mount, at the south end of St Mary Street. It moved to the Golate site in the early 1870s, in time for the *Western Mail* staff to organise, with the help of their readers, soup kitchens for striking miners, whose side they surprisingly took against the coal owners.

Early in the twenty-first century the newspapers were taken over by Trinity, the owners of the *Daily Mirror*. By this time Thomson House was also the home of Celtic Press, publishers of nine weekly newspapers in the South Wales Valleys, and the *Cardiff Post* and *Barry Post* – two free newspapers.

1961

Saints and Sinners

There was a religious flavour about 1961, the year that Cardiff City Council paid £206,000 to the Marquess of Bute for the site where the ruins of the thirteenth-century friary stood in Greyfriars Road (right). It was also the year that the first Lutheran church opened in Cardiff. The church, at Fairwater Green, was the fifteenth Lutheran church to open in Britain and the first Pastor was the Revd Marvin Brammirer, of Illinois who had arrived in Cardiff with his wife two years earlier.

Bishop Sante Uberto Barbieri took time off from a Methodist conference in Liverpool to make a special plea at a rally at Cathays Methodist church. The leading Methodist in Argentina, Bolivia and Uruguay was looking for a pastor to serve the 10,000 Welsh speakers in the Chubut Valley of Patagonia – the descendants of Welsh emigrants who went there in the mid-nineteenth century.

The Archbishop of Cardiff, the Most Revd Michael McGrath, died in February 1961 after leading Roman Catholics in Wales for twenty-one years. He was succeeded by Archbishop John Aloysius Murphy, who was enthroned at St David's Cathedral, Cardiff, on 31 October 1961 and who retired in 1983 – the year after he had welcomed Pope John Paul II to Cardiff.

The days when a bookie's runner could be found on many street corners were over when betting shops were made legal and there was a referendum in Wales like no other in the world. People went to the polls to decide whether or not pubs should open on Sundays for the first time since 1881. The nation was divided, with some areas remaining dry and others, including Cardiff, going wet. Similar polls were held every seven years until the pubs throughout Wales were allowed to open on Sundays. It was also the year that the city's first major bingo club, the Coliseum in Cowbridge Road, opened.

Harry Sherman, who with his brother Abraham founded Sherman Football Pools in Cardiff, died in 1961. The Sherman name was one of the first to go above the legal betting shops in the city, and it was a Sherman endowment that funded the theatre which carries the family name.

Cardiff solicitor Leo Abse caused a sensation when he arrived at the House of Commons on Budget Day, 17 April 1961, dressed in Edwardian style, including a stovepipe hat. The Labour MP for Pontypool said that after gazing at the sartorial sloth of the Tories for twelve months, he felt it was necessary to teach them how to dress. He stayed loyal to one of the biggest factories in his constituency, British Nylon spinners, by wearing a nylon shirt, socks and tie!

One of the city's oldest pubs, The Oxford, in The Hayes, Cardiff, closed after serving thirsty Cardiffians for 160 years. It was one of the last buildings to go to make way for the redevelopment part of the Central Area, including the Oxford Arcade, which was built on the site of the old hostelry. The hosts in the last years were Percy Williams and his wife, Elizabeth.

In a year when Cardiff was designated an army saluting base for 22-gun royal salutes, the city continued to change. Cyncoed Training College and the first multi-storey car park, in Greyfriars Road, were built. The Gaumont Cinema (formerly the Empire) in Queen Street and the Regent Cinema in Ely closed. The last Taff Swim was held at Roath Park, and the first match under floodlights was played at Ninian Park.

1962

Smallpox Outbreak

Smallpox, the disease that killed 300 million people throughout the world in the twentieth century, brought terror to people in Cardiff and South Wales in the early months of 1962. The contagious virus was brought to the city by a traveller from Pakistan, who came to Cardiff by train from Birmingham on 11 January 1962. Four other carriers who travelled on the same flight to Britain made for Bradford and Leeds. They, like South Wales, were all hit by a minor smallpox epidemic. But the fear of a major outbreak was so great that 900,000 South Wales men, women and children were vaccinated between January and April 1962. There was a total of forty-six cases in the Valleys and towns, but only one case in Cardiff where the trail started.

While a massive search was launched for anyone who may have been in contact with the traveller, or with any of the other victims, massive queues, up to a mile long, formed outside clinics in Cardiff and the Valleys. They ignored warnings that being vaccinated with cowpox, a method discovered by Edward Jenner in 1778, could be dangerous. At least fifteen people in Britain, including some in South Wales, died as a result of vaccination complications in the 1962 outbreak. Sadly, one of the victims of the disease in Wales was a pathologist who had carried out a post-mortem on an infected person.

A smallpox vaccination clinic was set up on a Llanrumney estate in January 1962.

What happened in Cardiff, Leeds and Bradford alerted the World Health Organisation (WHO) to the increased danger that smallpox was no longer something that occurred only in the Third World. It was now only a flight away from major centres of population in the developed world. A massive vaccination programme was carried out throughout the world, and the WHO announced that the disease had been eradicated. The Cardiff experience had helped to bring this about.

The *South Wales Echo* was always first with the news of any new case of smallpox in its area. This was made possible by its Rhondda reporter Oscar Rees who later revealed his source of information. He used to place bets with a street bookie near the ambulance station in Porth. Only one ambulance was dedicated to carrying smallpox suspects, and every time it left its depot the bookie tipped off Oscar by telephone.

The original colours of the 1st Battalion of the Welsh Guards were laid up in Llandaff Cathedral for a second time in January 1962. Guards with fixed bayonets escorted the colours into the Cathedral to the stirring tune of 'Men of Harlech' where the Dean of Llandaff, the Revd Eryl S. Thomas, received them from Col H.D.M. Dismsdale. The colours were salvaged after a parachute had ripped of the roof and damaged the interior of the cathedral during an air raid on 2/3 January 1941.

1963

Shadow of the Gallows

While MPs debated whether or not to end capital punishment in Britain, Edgar Valentine Black was sentenced to death on 7 October 1963 for shooting Richard Cook, whom he believed was his wife's lover. Richard Cook was shot with a sawn-off shotgun on the doorstep of his home in Llandudno Road, Rumney, Cardiff. Black, who had driven to Cardiff from his home in Stockton in a three-wheeled invalid car, had his appeal turned down by High Court judges and the execution at Cardiff Prison was set for 8 November. Two days before, the Home Secretary intervened and reduced the sentence to life imprisonment. The family of Richard Cook, especially his mother, believed that Black should have died on the gallows. He in fact died in prison more than twenty-five years later.

Cardiff man Richard Cook (far left) was murdered by Edgar Valentine Black. Cook had been having an affair with Mrs Edith Black and was shot by his assailant at his home in Llandudno Road, June 1963.

Following the assassination of America's President John F. Kennedy on 23 November 1963, a requiem mass, presided over by Archbishop John Murphy, was held at St David's Cathedral, Cardiff, where the future President had attended mass in 1938.

❖   ❖   ❖

There was drama at sea in 1963 when the passenger liner the *Laconia*, with 1,000 people on board, caught fire off the island of Madeira. Fifteen Cardiff people were among the thirty-four Welsh passengers on board; fortunately they all survived after a massive rescue operation.

❖   ❖   ❖

This was the year that the Beatles played to a packed house at the Capital Cinema, and when Cardiff-born jazz pianist Alex Templeton died. The last steam trains ran from Cardiff to London, and the subway linking Ferry Road to Cogan was closed. The Bishop of Llandaff School was officially opened.

1964

Salute to Tenovus

A charity registered in Cardiff in 1964 has raised millions of pounds to fight cancer and to boost many other worthwhile causes. The charity is Tenovus, which was stronger than ever as the city celebrated its 100th anniversary. There is a fascinating story as to how the organisation was formed nineteen years before it officially became a charity. In 1943, the year of the last air-raid on Cardiff, a haulage contractor named Eddie Price received multiple injuries when a lathe he was delivering for the Wartime Supply Ministry fell on top of him. He was unconscious in Cardiff Royal Infirmary for ten days and took several months to recover. One of his visitors was a 'man from the Pru' (Prudential), insurance manager David R. Edwards, who remembered how Eddie had come to his rescue when he ran out of petrol. He gave Eddie a portable radio, which he was not allowed to play as it would have disturbed other patients. With the help of eight other Cardiff businessmen, Eddie and David raised £1,200 in a year to buy headphones for every bed in the CRI. A link was made to Ninian Park, from where commentaries of football matches were relayed to the hospital. The ten men, who had the full backing of their wives, met monthly and named themselves the 'TENOVUS'. They were David Edwards, Eddie Price, C. Harris, G. Brinn, C. Rolfe, D. Curitz, G. Addis, H. Thomas, H. Gosling and T. Curitz. Paddy Ginn was also one of the original gang but as a policeman was not allowed to serve on the committee.

One could fill a book almost as big as this with the causes that have been supported by Tenovus since 1943. The trustees and directors over more than sixty

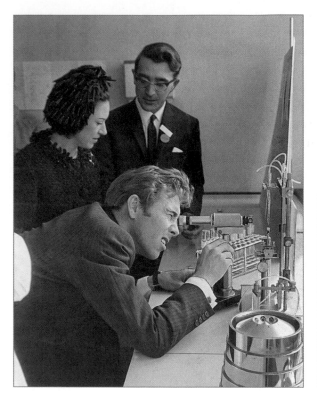

Lord Snowdon looks through a cathetometer at the Tenovus Institute for Cancer Laboratories at the Heath, while Dr K. Griffiths, Institute Superintendent, talks to Princess Margaret who opened the new building on14 April 1967.

Princess Margaret unveils the plaque commemorating the opening of the Tenovus Institute.

years acknowledge that they could not have achieved what they have without the dedication of their workers and volunteers and the generosity of the general public and businesses. They have all done Cardiff and Wales proud.

One of Wales' greatest athletes, Lynn Davies, leapt to long jump gold at the 1964 Olympic Games in Tokyo. He went on to add the European and Commonwealth titles to his collection two years later. His British record of 8.23 metres stood from 1968 to 2002.

Pensioner Courcy Cadogan became the first motorist to be fined in Cardiff after being reported by one of the new traffic wardens employed in the city. Courcy, of Bwlch Road, Fairwater, who was fined £2, was the only driver to appear in court. Seventeen other drivers pleaded guilty by letter.

England's cricket test captain Ted Dexter was selected by the Conservatives to challenge James Callaghan in Cardiff South-East, a marginal seat in 1964. Callaghan had a majority of less than 900 in the previous General Election, and the Tories, especially the chairman G.V. Wynne-Jones, were hoping that a sporting personality like Dexter could defeat the future Labour Prime Minister. They could not have been more wrong. Callaghan increased his majority to more than 7,000. As one commentator said at the time, the Tories picked the wrong sport: had they chosen long jump golden boy Lynn Davies or a Welsh rugby hero, they may have won the day.

The Welsh Office had been established in Cathays Park, Cardiff, two months before Labour took power. Their first Welsh Secretary was Jim Griffiths, who was followed by Cledwyn Hughes, who was succeeded by George Thomas.

The Maltese community mourned the death in 1964 of the man who was their friend and leader for nearly fifty years. Michael Camilleri acted as unofficial Maltese consul in the city from 1918. He became an adopted son of Cardiff at the end of the First World War during which he served in the Merchant Navy. He ran a seamen's hostel in Loudon Square, Butetown.

When the Second World War started he was on holiday in Malta with his family, but arrangements were made for him to return to Cardiff immediately because of his status in the city. When Malta was under siege, resulting in the island being awarded the George Cross, Michael's morale-boosting broadcasts were relayed by the BBC from Cardiff to his homeland. He later ran the George Cross Club in Cardiff and raised thousands of pounds for Maltese charities.

A relative of one of the most evil men in history came to Cardiff in 1964 in search of a peaceful place to settle. Karl Kramer was the nephew of a leading Nazi, Joseph Kramer, who commanded the notorious Belsen concentration camp in Germany where thousands of people died. Karl Kramer was only six years of age when his uncle was hanged for his war crimes, but he confided to friends in Cardiff that what he learnt in later life weighed heavily on his conscience. Karl, who was both deaf and dumb, was 36 when he arrived in Cardiff and lodged with a family in Arabella Street, Roath. He communicated with Beatrice Williams and her son-in-law by writing messages on a notepad.

Using hand signing he told his story to Hector Feeney, who was superintendent of the Mission for the Deaf in Windsor Place, Cardiff. Before coming to Cardiff, Karl had worked as a labourer with a circus in Ireland where he believed that people hated him for his uncle's sins. In 1965 he left his lodgings and all his belongings and never returned. No one in Cardiff knows what happened to him, but Hector Feeney suspected that he had fled the city after someone found out about his past.

Major changes took place at Cardiff Docks in 1964. The Bute West Dock closed on 31 January, and the last shipment of coal left Queen Alexandra Docks on 25 August. The restoration of Llandaff Cathedral, badly damaged in a 1941 air raid, was completed in 1964, the year the Cardiff Polyphonic Choir was founded.

1965

Churchill's Death

Sir Winston Churchill's death on 24 January 1965 was marked in Cardiff by tributes and memorial services. Representatives of the Council were present at the lying-in-state at Westminster and also at the State funeral, on the day when schools, shops and many offices were closed. Flags flew at half mast, and people recalled Prime Minister Churchill's visit to Cardiff in April 1941, when he saw for himself the damage caused by German bombs.

They also remembered him being cheered through the streets of Cardiff when he was made a Freeman of the City. Older residents were willing to forget that he was the man who had sent troops into Cardiff during the crippling seamen's strike in 1911.

❖   ❖   ❖

The Hennessys, a folk group which has done much to put Cardiff on the map, made its debut in the city in 1965. Frank Hennessy, Dave Burns and Paul Powell got together in the Central Boys Club, which stood on the corner of Bute Street. They were encouraged by the late Bill Barret, headmaster of Gladstone School and one of the city's greatest historians. He entered the Hennessys in a Cardiff City Council talent competition, Spotlight on Youth. The group won its section and the prize was a place in a gala concert at the New Theatre. It was the start of a glorious career that was still flourishing as the city prepared to celebrate its centenary.

❖   ❖   ❖

When the Beatles were awarded OBEs in the honours list in 1965, a Cardiff war hero was so angry he sent his MBE and citation back to Buckingham Palace. Merchant Navy Captain David Rees enjoyed listening to the Beatles on the radio at his home in Grangetown but was disgusted that they had been honoured by the Queen. He felt it cheapened awards such as his, which had been bestowed in 1940 for distinguished service during nearly forty years at sea. Ironically the Beatles decided later that they had made a mistake in accepting their MBEs as it linked them too closely to Prime Minister Harold Wilson and the Labour Party. They sent their medals back to the government.

Retired sea captain David Rees returned his MBE in protest at the award of OBEs to pop group the Beatles.

In a year when the Welsh language was officially given equal validity to English, the pure 'Care-diff' language was also in the news. Frank Hennessy speaks Welsh and is also a past master of the 'Care-diff' language. One wonders if he was one of the little horrors referred to in this letter which appeared in the *South Wales Echo* postbag. It was from Horace Dowling, of Cardiff:

> As a qualified elocutionist, I have been astonished by the number of parents who have sent their children to me with this pathetic plea. 'Please do something to rid him of this awful Cardiff accent.'
>
> They [the parents] will tell me: 'He will say orright for all right and he will persist in talking about Care-diff Air-ms Pair-k. And at Christmas he was invited to many pair-ties.'
>
> Yes, we all hear it and very ugly it is. But what can we expect when a few of their schoolteachers also talk Care-diffy?

Cardiff West MP George Thomas, later given the title of Viscount Tonypandy, was not the only politician linked to Cardiff to occupy the Speaker's Chair in the House of Commons. In the autumn of 1965, Liberal MP Roderic Bowen, QC was elected as deputy chairman of the Ways and Means Committee, which meant he was deputy to the Speaker. At the time of his appointment Mr Bowen was Recorder of Cardiff.

1966

Suffer the Little Children

An alarm clock that had stopped at 9.16 a.m. on 21 October 1966 provided vital evidence as to the exact time that an avalanche of colliery waste, known as shale, destroyed Ynys Owen Junior School and neighbouring houses in the South Wales mining village of Aberfan.

The clock was found by Michael Flynn, a volunteer, who later became a city councillor. At the time of the disaster Michael was a member of St John Ambulance Bridge and also of the Territorial Army in Cardiff. Michael, the brother of Labour MP Paul Flynn, gave evidence at the public inquiry into the Aberfan disaster, which resulted in the deaths of 144 people, including 116 children.

A major emergency plan was put into operation less than an hour after the disaster. One of the first units to arrive in the village, 18 miles north of Cardiff, was the Civil Defence group based at Whitchurch. Fr Patrick Kerrisk, who later became parish priest of the Holy Family Church, Fairwater, Cardiff, had arrived in the mining village only seven days before disaster struck. Eleven of his parishioners, ten of them children, died in the tragedy. They were among eighty-one victims buried in a mass grave at Aberfan. While the village and the world wept for the victims, a row broke out over a decision to use some of the money collected for the bereaved and injured to clear the remaining tips above the village. A deputation of parents lobbied the Welsh Office in Cardiff to protest, and when their pleadings fell on deaf ears Stephen Owen Davies, the veteran Labour MP for Merthyr, left the meeting in tears. The village had to wait more than thirty years before the money taken from the fund was returned to them.

John O'Sullivan, the co-author of this book, was the *Daily Mail*'s main reporter at the disaster and lived in the village for eleven weeks.

❖   ❖   ❖

Professor Colin Buchanan's blueprint for Cardiff was published in 1966, and the shape of the city by the end of the twentieth century was largely due to his vision. The report, which laid out a pattern for new roads and called for the redevelopment of the city centre, was greeted with mixed feelings. There were protests at his suggestion that St David's Cathedral, in Charles Street, should be demolished. It was saved and became the cornerstone of St David's Centre and St David's Hall. His most sensational idea, to exhume 30,000 bodies from Cathays Cemetery to make way for a new road, was also rejected.

❖   ❖   ❖

The fate of Newtown, Cardiff's Little Ireland, was decided in 1966, when the City Council agreed to demolish the houses in the area which was created for refugees from the Great Irish Famine in the 1840s. Light industry was established on the site.

❖   ❖   ❖

Neil and Glenys Kinnock seen here walking with the miners in Cardiff, 1977.

Neil Kinnock, who was to become leader of the Labour Party, a European Commissioner and a life peer, was at the centre of a major row at Cardiff University's Student Union in 1966. He resigned his post as president of the Union and walked out with his executive committee, which included his future wife, Glenys Parry, who went on to be elected as a Euro MP for the part of Wales covering Cardiff. The dispute was over the choice of delegates for the annual conference of the National Union of Students.

Thirty-three years after quitting his Union post, Neil Kinnock returned to the place from which he had graduated, as President of the University itself. He succeeded Lord Crickhowell, who had held the post for ten years. Neil, who opted for the title of Lord Kinnock of Bedwellty, took his seat in the House of Lords on 31 January 2005.

One of Cardiff's most popular entertainers, bandleader Wally Bishop, stage name 'Waldini', died on 6 January 1966. During the Second World War he led an ENSA group which performed in battle zones in many parts of the world. In peacetime his band played at dance halls in Cardiff.

1967

Bomb at Temple of Peace

Welsh extremists were blamed for a bomb that damaged the Temple of Peace in Cardiff in November. The blast caused damage, but fortunately there were no casualties. Extra police were brought in to control demonstrators demanding a better deal for the Welsh language. Around this time, activists also painted out English-only road signs throughout the city. BBC Two was able to screen the demonstration in colour, which had been available to Cardiff for three months. BBC Wales had moved from Park Place to Llandaff in March 1967, when Princess Margaret opened the new building

A bomb was also planted at the Inland Revenue skyscraper in Llanishen the following year. Again it was damage only and no casualties.

Cardiff is no stranger to industrial disputes, but the one at Mount Stuart Dry Dock in 1967 had a rare twist. The story started in February 1965, when the workers demanded their foreman 'Big Mick' Reardon be dismissed before ending a thirteen-day strike. They claimed that Big Mick, a 42-year-old, twenty-stone former Welsh Guardsman, was a 'boss's man' who was too tough as a supervisory chargehand.

After losing his £37 a week job, Reardon kept his wife and two children on just £10 a week benefit money. Then came a call almost unique in industrial relations. The dry dock workers wanted Big Mick back – to lead their fight against a productivity agreement that, ironically, included a clause which would have allowed Reardon to get his own job back. The men went on unofficial strike for ten days, and when they returned to work they found that the firm had taken on 100 outsiders, which put all their jobs at risk.

Reardon showed what a big man he really was when he forgot the hate of his former workmates to fight for the cause. The cry went round the docks: 'Big Mick is back'. One man at a dockside meeting told Mick that he still hated him, but accepted he was the only man to lead their battle. Big Mick agreed and helped to bring peace to the dry docks where he was eventually reinstated in his old job. The men knew he had good reason to have crossed the picket line while they were on strike, but the giant of a man believed in the cause for which the men were fighting.

This was the year that the Greyfriars ruins were demolished to make way for the multi-storey Pearl Building. Not far away, in Park Place, the tower block of the University was completed. The winders no longer had to climb up the clock tower at the City Hall, as an automatic system had been installed. In a year when Glamorgan Cricket Club started playing at their new ground at Sophia Gardens, two great sportsmen were born: hurdler Colin Jackson and diving champion Robert Morgan. Another who made his debut in the world was Huw Bunford, who became a singer with the Super Furry Animals.

1968

Redevelopment Plan

Plans to redevelop the Cardiff Central area were revealed at a press conference on 6 February 1968 by the City Planning Officer Ewart Parkinson. He said the aim of the Council and its partner, the Ravenseft Group, was to create a regional shopping, entertainment, cultural and commercial centre that would bear comparison with any in the United Kingdom. Anyone looking at Cardiff as it celebrated its 100th year as a city would accept that the dream of 1968 had been realised.

The Council envisaged capital spending of £70 million to achieve its goal; a tremendous investment for future generations and one matching that of the fledging city of Cardiff, which in the early twentieth century made the Civic Centre one of the finest in the world. Ewart Parkinson, who had planned the rebuilding of the badly bombed City of Plymouth before coming to Cardiff, was optimistic about his scheme for the capital of Wales. 'The people of this city can achieve wonderful things,' he said. 'The opportunities are there if only we can work together to secure them.' There is no doubt that his optimism was well placed.

American Mark Spitz is one of the swiftest and greatest swimmers of all time. In the 1972 Olympic Games in Munich he won a total of seven gold medals. But four years earlier, at the Olympic Games in Mexico, he finished a poor eighth in a 200-metre butterfly race in which Martyn Woodroffe, of Cardiff, won the silver medal. Two years later Martyn, a member of the City of Cardiff Welsh squad, won silver in the

200-metre butterfly, bronze in the 200-metre medley and a second bronze in the 200-metre medley relay

Martyn started swimming when he was at Waterhall School but was a sixth former at Canton High School when he struck silver. He spent some time as Director of Swimming for Scotland before taking up a post as Coaching Coordinator with the Amateur Swimming Association. He coached over fifty British, English, Welsh and Scottish senior and junior internationals and representatives at every major championships and games. As Cardiff celebrated its 100th anniversary as a city, he was hands-on Coaching Coordinator for Wales working with clubs, coaches and swimmers both in their home programmes and with national squads.

Martyn Woodroffe's victory over Mark Spitz came in a year when Cardiff's greatest Olympian, Paulo Radmilovic, died at Weston-super-Mare. 'Raddy' took part in six Olympic Games and won four gold medals for water polo.

The first Alcoholics Anonymous group was founded in Cardiff in 1968 by a priest who was drinking as many as sixteen bottles of spirits a week and who had lived rough for sixteen years after being banned from his religious duties in his native Northern Ireland. Fr John McLoughin gave up drinking in 1965 and remained dry until his death at St Winifrid's Hospital, Cardiff, in 1998. During that time he was friend and counsellor to hundreds of people who suffered from alcoholism; he made a tape recording of his story and sent it to people all over the world. In 1967 he was accepted as a priest in the Archdiocese of Cardiff and served parishes in Ely and Leckwith. His door and heart were always open to those who had problems through drink, and he was respected and loved by people from all walks of life who sought his help.

In a year when George Thomas became Secretary of State for Wales, Cardiff's new police station opened in Cathays Park; HTV succeeded TWW as the Cardiff-based commercial television station and the SS *Columbialand*, a Swedish vessel, was the largest ship to berth at Cardiff in the history of the docks.

1969

Investiture Year

The Queen kept her promise made at the end of the Empire Games in Cardiff in 1958 to invest her son, Charles, as Prince of Wales. The ceremony took place at Caernarfon Castle when Cardiff's elegantly dressed Lord Mayor, Lincoln Hallinan, represented the city.

After the investiture, the new Prince of Wales toured the Principality, and when he visited Cardiff he switched on the fountains in front of the City Hall, installed to commemorate the occasion. The sprays of the fountain are in the form of the Prince of Wales Feathers. Prince Charles was granted the Freedom of the City.

❖   ❖   ❖

Jimmy Wilde, one of the greatest boxers of all time, died in Cardiff on 10 March. Known as the 'Mighty Atom', the 'Tylorstown Terror' and the 'Ghost with a Hammer in his Hand', Wilde lost only four of his 149 fights between 1910 and 1923, fifteen of which were no-decision bouts. In an incredible four-year period he was undefeated in 101 fights.

Jimmy was born in Quakers Yard in 1892 and started working as a miner in Tylorstown when he was twelve. From the age of 16 he did his apprenticeship as a fighter in the boxing booths run in Cardiff by Jack Scarrott. In 1912 he turned down a chance to visit America. Wilde served as a sergeant instructor in the First World War and was crowned flyweight champion of the world at the age of 24 in 1916. He retired in 1923 after losing his world title to Filipino fighter Pancho Villa in New York. Jimmy remained a celebrity in Wales for the rest of his life and often enjoyed a game of snooker in the Queens Hotel.

Cardiff boxer Jimmy Wilde was World Flyweight Champion between 1916 and 1923.

Jimmy would have been proud of Eddie Avoth, who thrilled boxing fans in his home city of Cardiff when he knocked out John McCormack in the eleventh round to win the British light-heavyweight championship. He added the Commonwealth Crown the following year when he knocked out Trevor Thornberry in the sixth round. Avoth lost both titles in 1971 when he was knocked out by Chris Finnegan in the closing minutes of a gruelling fifteen-round bout.

❖   ❖   ❖

Mother Teresa (left), the Missionaries of Charity founder who has been acclaimed as a modern-day saint, visited St Cadoc's School, Llanrumney, Cardiff, on her first visit to Britain, in 1969. She included the school on her itinerary because the children and staff had raised £1,500 for her order, which looks after homeless people and beggars in Calcutta.

This was the year that Cardiff City Police and the Glamorgan Constabulary merged to form the South Wales Police, and when solicitor Manuel Delgado became the first non-white magistrate in Cardiff. Dafydd Hughes became the first Plaid Cymru member of Cardiff City Council when he was elected for Plasmawr. The Welsh National Opera Company moved to its new headquarters in John Street and Glamorgan won cricket's County Championship.

1970

River Out of Eden

Novelist Jack Jones, who died at the age of 86 in 1970, used to cycle from his home in Rhiwbina to Cardiff Central Library where he did research for his books, which reflect a great deal of the history of Cardiff and South Wales. His best-known books are *River Out of Eden*, the river being the Taff and the plot based on the development of Cardiff, and *Off to Philadelphia in the Morning*, which told the story of the composer Joseph Parry, one of the greatest Welsh musicians of the nineteenth century.

Parry's opera *Blodwen* was performed over 500 times in Wales, England and America. His love song 'Myfanwy' remains a favourite and is known all over the world, as are his famous hymn tunes including 'Aberystwyth'. Parry was born in Merthyr and died in Penarth, where he is buried in St Augustine's churchyard.

After serving in the First World War, Jack Jones followed many professions and stood as a Liberal candidate for parliament before writing *Rhondda Roundabout*, which was published in 1934.

Trolleybuses, which needed long poles to be manoeuvred to help them around corners, stopped operating on the streets of Cardiff on 11 January 1970. The last journey was from the Pier Head to Mill Lane. In March 1970 conductors were made redundant when one-man/woman buses were introduced; passengers dropped the right money in a sealed box and no change was given.

This was the year that the first game was played at the Arms Park, which had been revamped within the development of the neighbouring National Ground which also opened in 1970. An Aer Lingus Boeing 737 made history when it became the first pure jet airliner to land at Cardiff Airport, Rhoose.

The Pearl Tower, later renamed the Capital Tower, was built on the old Greyfriars site and the Bute East Dock closed.

1971

Royal Opening

The University Hospital of Wales, also known as the Heath, was opened by the Queen in November 1971. The UHW is one of the top teaching hospitals in Britain, and staff there deal with 5,000 outpatients, 500 day patients and 200 day patients a week. The hospital comes under the umbrella of the Cardiff and Vale Trust, which oversees all NHS hospitals in the area.

As promised by Conservative Minister of Transport Ernest Marples four years earlier, when challenged by the deputy editor of the *South Wales Echo*, Eastern Avenue was completed and so was the flyover at North Road. The Duke of Edinburgh also cut a ribbon in the city that year when he opened the University Music Department in Corbett Road.

Ping-pong diplomacy came to the world of sport and politics in 1971, and the credit for breaking through the Bamboo Curtain belongs to a Cardiff couple, Roy Evans and his wife, Nancy. Roy's role as general secretary and president (1967–87) of the International Table Tennis Federation took him to many corners of the world, including North and South Korea and China, where he was invited to meet the former Prime Minister Chou En-lai.

The man from Penylan, who had been introduced to table tennis at the Cardiff YMCA, was asked by the Chinese politician to arrange for players taking part in the world championships in Japan to visit China on their way home. Roy arranged for American players, accompanied by six American journalists, to visit Beijing. A couple of weeks later President Richard Nixon accepted an invitation to visit China and freely acknowledged that it was Roy's ping-pong diplomacy that had made this possible. Roy was awarded the OBE in the 1972 honours list and later became president of the International Table Tennis Federation. Throughout his term of office Roy was supported by his wife, Nancy, who was a top table tennis player from 1929 to 1947. Nancy was in her late nineties when she died, before Roy who passed away at the age of 88 in Cardiff on 19 May 1998.

Labour stalwart Jack Keohane should have been the Lord Mayor in 1971 but declined the honour, which was a great pity as he was a quietly spoken humble man who would have done the city proud. The man who did become Lord Mayor was Hugh Ferguson-Jones, a leading Conservative and a giant in local government. He was born at Caerwys in North Wales on 14 June 1913 and served through the Second World War as a navigating officer in the Merchant Navy. He left the sea in 1947 and went into partnership as an insurance broker with Glamorgan cricket captain Wilf Wooler, who had spent three years as a prisoner of the Japanese. 'Fergy', as he was known, was leader of the City Council before becoming Lord Mayor. He served on numerous committees and organisations. In his year of office he led the fight to preserve the status of the City of Cardiff as the capital of Wales at a time when local government reorganisation was taking place. He more than anyone encouraged the St David's Trust in its plans for a Welsh National Arts Centre in the city. Those who knew him would agree that St David's Hall, in The Hayes, is a monument to him. He died during a Council meeting on the eve of the honours list in which he was knighted. The honour was granted to him posthumously.

The idea of producing talking newspapers for the blind originated in Norway in the 1960s, spread to other parts of Scandinavia and was slowly introduced to Britain. In the early years there were only five talking newspapers or magazines in the United Kingdom and four of these were in Wales. The biggest one was the *South Wales Talking Magazine for the Blind*, produced for the first time in 1971 at the Institute for the Blind in Newport Road, Cardiff, by volunteers, including blind and partially sighted people. The enthusiasm of volunteers like founder vice-chairman Jack Treeby and secretary Bill Smith, both registered blind, did a great deal to make the project possible. More than thirty years later the magazine is still flourishing; one of its main presenters Alan George, has been blind from birth.

In 1971 Cardiff Rugby Club captain, Gerald Davies, played a starring role, scoring two tries in tests against New Zealand. The Lions won the series 2–1. The Cambridge Blue and Barbarian also scored twenty tries in the forty-six games he played for Wales.

Alan George, seen here with his mother, was born blind but became one of the main presenters with the *South Wales Talking Magazine for the Blind*.

1972

Exciting Chapter

Cardiff's Chapter Arts Centre was founded in Cardiff on St David's Day, 1 March 1972, four years after the idea had been floated by local artists Christine Kinsey and Brian Jones and journalist Mick Flood. They found a home for the centre at the old Canton High School on Market Street and staged a series of events to raise money and generate interest in the idea of an arts centre. Their events included a twelve-hour pop concert in Sophia Gardens with Pink Floyd topping the bill, with Black Sabbath and Quintessence in support.

Within a short space of time, painters, printmakers, sculptors, potters and other artists moved into the building. Amateur groups like the South Wales Arts Society and Everyman Theatre Company also joined the centre, and the Cardiff Cine Society led the way in the conversion of the old girls' cloakroom into one of the best small cinema spaces in South Wales. Classrooms were converted into a gallery the old school hall became a theatre. Moving Being, Cardiff Laboratory Theatre and Paupers Carnival moved in, and Chapter became a real focus for both artists and audiences.

Thirty years on, Chapter remained true to the original vision of its founders. A cultural and business success story, it housed many of Wales' best-known names in theatre, dance, art and animation. It has promoted a long list of famous names from film directors Justin Kerrigan and Chris Monger (a former Chapter board member) to Turner Prize-nominated artists Mona Hartoum and Cornelia Parker; from Oscar-nominated animators Joanna Quinn (who is based at Chapter) and the creator of Wallace and Gromit, Nick Park, to musicians John Cale and Susan Sontag; from comedians Jerry Sadowitz and Ben Elton to actors Willem Dafoe and former Monty Python star Terry Jones.

There was a minute's silence at football grounds throughout Britain following the death of former Cardiff City and Wales captain Fred Keenor, When Wales played Scotland at Ninian Park in 1924 both captains were Cardiff City players: Fred Keenor captained Wales, and Jimmy Blair was Scotland's skipper. Keenor was wounded twice in the First World War, but went on to win thirty-two caps for Wales. He also led City when they won the FA Cup in 1927.

This was the year that the Prince of Wales Orthopaedic Hospital in The Parade, Cardiff, closed and the filling-in of Bute West Dock was completed. The National Sports Centre in Sophia Gardens and the Posthouse Hotel in Eastern Avenue opened. The Wood Street Congregational Church and the first of the towers at Roath Power Station were demolished. The new passenger terminal was opened at Cardiff Airport, and Flat Holm was designated as a site of Special Scientific Interest. Howells store was taken over by the House of Fraser.

1973

Nobel Prize Winner

In 1973 an old boy of Cardiff High School, Brian D. Josephson, shared a Nobel Prize for Physics, at the age of 33. While studying for his Ph.D. at Cambridge in 1962, Brian Josephson predicted how an electrical current could flow between two superconductors (materials with zero electrical resistance) even when an insulator was placed between them. This became known as the Josephson effect, a phenomenon of such significance that it has entered scientific dictionaries. The theory has been applied to create extremely sensitive scientific instruments.

Professor Josephson, who was born in Cardiff on 4 January 1940, won a research fellowship at Trinity in 1962 and gained his Ph.D. two years later. He was elected a Fellow of the Royal Society in 1970 and was named a professor at Cambridge in 1974, the year after winning the Nobel Prize. Brian's late father, Abraham Josephson, was a French teacher at Howardian High School, Cardiff. His late mother, Mimi, was a freelance journalist and poet. Brian Josephson acknowledges the encouragement and help given to him at Cardiff High School by maths teacher Arthur G. Davies and physics master Emrys Jones. When not studying, Brian loved playing chess or going on cycle rides with his friends. He was also interested in astronomy and was a regular visitor to the former Penylan Observatory, a ten-minute walk from his home. Brian's parents moved from Cardiff to Cambridge in the 1980s, and the Professor has visited Cardiff only once in thirty years, to give a talk at an Institute of Physics conference. He enjoys visiting Snowdonia, now his main link with Wales. He says the work that won him the Nobel Prize has benefited the medical and scientific worlds and also possibly quantum computers.

The connection between advanced physics and the inner workings of the brain became the focus of Professor Josephson's controversial interest in the paranormal. His work in this field has been scorned by some other academics, but as his native city prepared to celebrate its centenary, the Cambridge University-based professor was continuing to seek a scientific basis for phenomena such as mental telepathy and spoon-bending. He insists that telepathy experiments have consistently produced results that cannot be explained by mere probability. His guiding principle is the Royal Society's motto *nullius in verba* – 'Take nobody's word for it.' He says he applies the motto to the people who state that such phenomena as mental telepathy and spoon-bending are absurd, and, equally, to people who state the reverse!

People power came to the fore with a vengeance in Cardiff in 1973 when a by-election result led to a controversial road scheme being axed by the city council. The Conservative-controlled council was fully expected to approve the Hook Road, which would have run from Caerphilly Road, through Roath and Adamsdown to link up with The Bay area. Two thousand houses had been compulsory-purchased and would have been demolished to make way for the road, which had been proposed in the Buchanan Plan. But it was not just the living but the dead who would have been affected had the Hook Road gone ahead. For it would have cut a swathe through Cathays Cemetery and the council was planning to clear 10,000 graves and re-inter 30,000 bodies in fields to the east of the city.

The Council was due to approve the scheme on a Monday, but a by-election in the true blue Penylan Ward the previous Thursday changed all that. Schoolteacher Yvette Roblin won the seat for Labour after campaigning on one issue: 'STOP THE HOOK ROAD'.

The then Conservative chairman of the planning committee, Ron Watkiss, listened to what the electorate had to say. On the Monday he moved that the Hook Road scheme go ahead – then abstained from voting, allowing the plan to be defeated by just one vote. The dead in Cathays Cemetery could rest in peace.

❖   ❖   ❖

This was the year the Sherman Theatre and the Bute Theatre, linked to the Welsh College of Music and Drama, opened, as did the first gallery at the Welsh Folk Museum at St Fagans and the skyscraper Inland Revenue office in Llanishen. Cardiff General Station was renamed Cardiff Central.

1974

Local Government Changes

Major changes in local government took place in 1974, the year that the ancient title of Alderman was abolished. Many of the functions, including education, which were previously carried out by Glamorgan County Council, were transferred to the City Council. Similar changes took place throughout Wales. Eventually the City of Cardiff became the City and County of Cardiff and moved its headquarters from the City Hall to the County Hall in Cardiff Bay, although offices continued to be maintained at the City Hall and in Wood Street, Cardiff. The first meeting of the new authority took place on 23 March 1974.

The Central Fire Station was transferred from Westgate Street to Adamsdown. Archaeologists carrying out a dig near the site of the demolished fire station, on the corner of Westgate Street and Quay Street, made an intriguing discovery in April 1974. They found more than twenty-seven Egyptian gold coins and about two dozen Spanish silver coins, which were said to have a total value of £10,000. There were no clues as to how the treasure trove came to be there but where they were found, on the site of the Welsh Sports outfitters in Quay Street, was close to where the River Taff used to flow before it was diverted away from what is now Westgate Street. The archaeologists from Brighton carried out a fingertip search of the site after the coins had been unearthed by an excavator. The owner of the demolition company decided to donate the find to the Victoria and Albert Museum in London.

This was the year when the first royal film première was held in Cardiff. Among the guests at the Olympia Cinema for the showing of *Murder on the Orient Express* were Prince Charles and the thriller writer Agatha Christie. The County Cinema in Rumney, the Queens Hotel in St Mary Street and the Rose and Crown all closed in 1974, the year that Brunei House, the biggest building in the city, was opened. Bilingual signs were erected at Queen Street station. The new Students Union opened in Park Place.

The site in Quay Street where ancient coins were found.

1975

International Twinning

Visitors to Cardiff are surprised to see a road with a French name in front of the City Hall. Boulevard de Nantes, which was dedicated in 1975, is a tribute to the successful twinning since 1963 with the French town of Nantes.

When it comes to twinning with overseas countries Cardiff is one of the front runners. The city has been twinned with Stuttgart in Germany since 1955 – the year that Cardiff was named as capital of Wales. Stuttgart is capital of Baden-Württemberg, in south-west Germany, and has a population of 588,617. It is at the heart of one of Germany's major industrial regions.

The next twinning agreement was signed in 1959 with Lugansk, Ukraine. Lugansk is a major road and rail hub situated on the eastern border of the country, on the northern slopes of the Donets'k mountain range. The city has a population of 522,000.

Xiamen in China was the next town to twin with Cardiff. When the link was made in 1983, it was the first of its kind between the United Kingdom and China.

Xiamen is situated on the south-east coast of the country and is a popular tourist destination. The long and strong links between Cardiff and Norway were cemented in 1996 when a twinning agreement was made with the Hordaland County Council. The population is 422,000 and the main town is Bergen, the second-largest city in Norway.

This was the year that the Roman Wall of the Castle was opened to the public for the first time; the first phase of pedestrianisation of Queen Street was introduced; the first bus lanes were marked in Queen Street and St Mary Street, motorists were able to use the new Clarence Bridge; and subways were available for pedestrians near the Civic Centre. The Japanese Panasonic Company at Pentwyn and Companies House in Cathays brought new employment to the City. The Welsh College of Music and Drama moved to its new site in North Road, some say to ensure that no road widening would take place along that route. Benson and Hedges showjumping was staged at the Castle, a tribute to Cardiff-born David Broome, one of Britain's greatest showjumpers, and F1 Powerboat racing was held at the East Bute Dock for the first time.

1976

Political Double

There was a political double for the city in 1976 when Jim Callaghan, MP for Cardiff South-East, became Prime Minister and his Labour colleague George Thomas, MP for Cardiff West was elected Speaker of the House of Commons. Both had represented their constituencies since 1945. Callaghan had been Foreign Minister and Chancellor of the Exchequer before he occupied 10 Downing Street. He failed to win the 1979 General Election, which the Conservatives won under the leadership of Margaret Thatcher. The Conservatives remained in power for eighteen years ending Jim Callaghan's hopes of returning to the front bench of government. He was elevated to the House of Lords, and as Cardiff celebrated its 100th anniversary Lord Callaghan was in his ninety-third year. He died in 2005.

George Thomas, a former Secretary of State for Wales and Home Office Minister, remained as Speaker after the Tories came to power. He made history when his command 'Order, Order' rang out when radio and television were allowed to broadcast House of Commons debates. He was respected by all sides of the House and was given the title of Viscount Tonypandy when he retired from the Commons. He died in 1997. Both men had been made Freemen of Cardiff in 1975.

This was the year that Crown Prince Akihito of Japan visited Cardiff, and the Sealed Knot Society re-enacted the Battle of St Fagans. The first open day was held at Cardiff Wales Airport and the 125-Intercity service was launched between Cardiff and London. The Welsh National Opera Company staged its first production at the Sherman Theatre; six months later the opera company's props were destroyed in a fire at their store at Roath coal depot. The first triple-screen cinema, the ABC, opened in Queen Street, and the new Salvation Army hostel opened in Bute Street. The frigate HMS *Llandaff* was decommissioned, and the death took place of Cardiff's David Jacobs, who won a gold medal at the 1912 Olympics.

1977

Buller Sullivan

Jim Buller Sullivan, the most prodigious goal-kicker the game of Rugby League has ever seen, died in September 1977. In his 928 first-class matches Cardiff-born Sullivan kicked 2,687 goals, including 160 in internationals. In a record number of 774 appearances for his club Wigan, he kicked 2,317 goals. He also got 96 tries during his twenty-five years' playing career.

His record of 22 goals and 44 points scored in a Challenge Cup match has stood for over seventy years. He made a record 60 international appearances, 25 of them for Great Britain in test matches against Australia and New Zealand. His international totals of 160 goals and 329 points are also records.

He was a fine all-round fullback and a great leader who captained Great Britain in fifteen tests and led the Ashes-winning 1932 Tourists to Australasia, appearing in all six test matches, three in Australia and three in New Zealand.

Cardiff, like every other city in Britain, has its share of homeless people. Boxing Day lunches were provided for these men and women at Tredegarville Baptist church hall, in Roath and the event in 1977 resulted in a remarkable outcome for one of the guests, 'Don the Dosser'. After lunch he went on the stage, sat at the piano and played classical pop, jazz and sing-a-long music like a professional. A report in 'The Stroller' column of the *South Wales Echo* led to a call from the landlord of the Graig Hotel in Newport, who wanted Don to entertain his customers on New Year's Eve. He knew he was taking a chance, for Don had lost his job as a top engineer on the Kariba Dam in Africa as well as his wife and children and home because of his drink problem. But Don was a great success at the Newport pub and managed to stay sober on the Saturday nights and Sunday lunchtimes that he played there.

From Monday to Friday he dossed in derelict houses or under railway arches, spending whatever money he had on drink. He only missed one weekend at the pub. That was when he got drunk and slept in a railway wagon at Canton sidings, in Cardiff. He woke up near Preston and had to hitchhike back to Cardiff! Don's fame as a pianist spread and sometimes he performed at a variety of social events including a party for disabled children. The organisers gave Don £5, which he immediately spent on a half bottle of whisky. But let Don take up the story:

Suddenly I thought of those poor children whose bodies were twisted and broken through no fault of their own. And there was I destroying myself with drink. I hurled the unopened bottle of whisky into the River Taff and with the help of a probation officer, who had been looking after me since I had been in jail, I was given a home at Dyfrig House, which catered for alcoholics. It was not easy, but I stayed there and stayed sober for two years, slowly but surely crawling out of the gutter with the help of the other residents and the staff and friends of Dyfrig House. The Ex-Prisoners Aid Society took an interest in me and I was lucky enough to find a good job in London.

A good job was an understatement. Don, who once worked on the Concorde engines at Rolls-Royce and helped to commission part of the Aberthaw Power Station in South Wales, was appointed the senior technician in the electronics engineering department of Queen Mary's University, earning around £15,000 a year.

In 1984 Don was interviewed by Steve Taylor for a Radio Wales and Radio Four programme. His ex-mother-in-law, who lived in the north of England, heard the programme and through the BBC invited Don to visit her. His former wife had remarried, but he accepted the invitation. His joy was complete when he was unexpectedly reunited with his son and daughter, whom he had last seen in Africa when they were little more than babies fourteen years earlier. Don retired to live near his family, full of gratitude for the people of Cardiff for rescuing him from the gutter. He remained dry and whenever he played the piano he ended his recital with his own particular theme song – 'I Did it My Way'!

This was the year that Cardiff City Council and the Heron Corporation signed a £22-million-pound deal for the redevelopment of land south of Queen Street, the site that became St David's Centre. Seccombes Store and The Taff Vale, the last pub in Queen Street, closed. Forty-eight years after a passenger liner service started between Cardiff and Canada, direct flights from Cardiff Airport to Toronto were inaugurated. Jim Callaghan opened the Welsh Industrial and Maritime Museum in Bute Place, and Southgate House in Wood Street also opened, on the site of the former Wood

Street Congregational Church (left). The M4 links between St Mellons and Tredegar Park and Coryton to Pencoed were both completed. The last greyhound races took place at Cardiff Arms Park on 30 July, and the first Royal Command Performance was held at the New Theatre in December.

1978

Cry Freedom

A former *Western Mail* sub-editor arrived back in Britain on New Year's Day 1978, a national and international hero: Donald Woods, who was banned in his own country of South Africa for using the *Daily Dispatch*, the newspaper he founded and edited, to fight apartheid. He escaped South Africa in the guise of a priest and used his knowledge and journalistic skills to bring the evil policy of apartheid to the attention of the world. The blockbuster film *Cry Freedom* was based on his book which told his story and of his relationship with Steve Biko, a leader of South Africa's Black Consciousness movement who died in detention after being tortured by security police.

Woods ran the *Daily Dispatch* for eleven years before being placed under house arrest. From the time he arrived back in Britain in 1978 he campaigned for South African democracy through lecture tours and news articles. He did as much as anyone to secure the release from prison of Nelson Mandela and the eventual collapse of the apartheid system that made South African Blacks second-class citizens in their own country.

In his first year of freedom Woods became the first private citizen to address the UN Security Council. The man, who worked as a sub-editor in Cardiff for ten months, toured the United States to promote the anti-apartheid movement, met President Jimmy Carter and spoke at Harvard University as a Nieman Fellow. He also served as a consultant on South Africa to the European Union and the Commonwealth of Britain and its former colonies. He always had a place in his heart for Cardiff, the city which he said made him so welcome. He was made a Commander of the British Empire before his death in August 2001.

This year was the crowning glory in the golden era of Welsh rugby, when Wales won the Grand Slam in Cardiff after winning six Triple Crowns. The Welsh team became legends in their own lifetime and comprised J.P.R. Williams, who could stop any opponent and whose speed put him in a class of his own; fast-moving Gerald Davies; bearded Ray Gravell, a powerful centre with the heart of a Welsh Dragon; Steve Fenwick, a great all-rounder; J.J. Williams, who could outrun most players; fly-half Phil Bennett, whose ability to jinx past players made him one of the greatest players of all time; Gareth Edwards, the finest scrum-half to don a rugby jersey; Derek Quinnell, a big, aggressive man in the back row; Terry Cobner, who was master of the maul; Jeff Squire and Allan Martin, both masters of the line-out; and finally, the legendary Pontypool front row, the most-feared trio in rugby history – Geoff Wheel, Graham Price and Bobby Windsor. Wales had to wait another twenty-seven years before winning the next Grand Slam.

One of Cardiff's greatest and best-loved chararacters, Victor Parker, died on 8 February 1978. A talented guitarist and folk-singer Victor, affectionately known as 'Narker Parker', entertained in The Quebec and other pubs in the Bute Street area. He was best known for his 'Chicken Song' but played a range of music that brought some of the experience from London jazz clubs to Cardiff. Naturally Victor was given a New Orleans-style send-off: an all-night wake was held at the Bute Town Community Centre before the funeral. Guitarists from all over South Wales made a wreath from plectrums which was placed on top of the coffin. Various groups played as the mourners danced the night away. There was one unforgettable moment when the master of ceremonies called for a big hand for the man in the box in the corner, 'without whom we would not be enjoying ourselves'. Headed by a jazz band, the coffin was carried by bearers through crowd-lined Bute Street from the community centre to St Mary the Virgin Church. After the service the band played 'When the Saints Go Marching In' as the crowd danced and sang in an outstanding tribute to an outstanding man.

Vic Parker's funeral procession in Bute Street.

This was the year that the Capitol, once the biggest cinema in Britain, closed. Many famous entertainers performed there, including the Beatles. Appropriately, when the National Eisteddfod was held at Pentwyn, Ysgol Glantaf, Cardiff's first Welsh-language comprehensive school opened. The Grangetown Stand at Ninian Park was demolished, as was the Drill Hall in Dumfries Place and Ebenezer Welsh Congregational Chapel, which stood on the site of St David's Arcade. The bodies from the chapel's graveyard were exhumed and re-interred at Cathays Cemetery, in a corner of the plot where 349 Irish victims of the 1850 cholera outbreak were laid to rest in a mass grave. The unmarked grave adjoins the public house on the corner of Wedal Road. The Welch Regiment Museum opened at Cardiff Castle, the first district leisure centre was established at Ely, and Transport House, the headquarters of the Welsh Labour Party and the Transport and General Workers Union, opened its doors on the corner of Cathedral Road and Cowbridge Road East.

1979

Steelworks Closed

The closure of Cardiff's East Moors Steelworks in 1979 resulted in the loss of 3,200 jobs – a body blow to a city where the docks were already in decline, with coal exports virtually at a halt. Protest marches were held in a vain bid to save the steelworks that had been the backbone of industry in the city for decades. The Splott area was developed to house the steelworkers, and it was this part of Cardiff that suffered most when the giant works closed. Unemployment was well above average for Britain and almost reached the depression levels of the 1930s.

Cardiff's industrial heritage was linked to the late eighteenth century when the Glamorganshire Canal was built to bring iron and coal down from the South Wales Valleys. The Taff Vale Railway was established in 1840, a year after the Bute West Dock, the first of many docks in Cardiff, was opened by the 2nd Marquess of Bute. It was the building of the docks that led to Cardiff becoming one of the most cosmopolitan places in the world, with nearly fifty different nationalities settled in the area.

The worst floods in Cardiff for more than two centuries caused major damage to the area west of the River Taff, on 27 December 1979. Those monitoring the fast-flowing river wrongly thought that the danger had passed when the high tidemark

Cowbridge Road under water in 1979.

had been reached without any serious problems. However, it was not a tidal flood but one resulting from the watershed of heavy rain from the previous two days entering the river from the streams on the Brecon Beacons, resulting in a trail of damage to villages and towns upstream. The river broke its banks at Llandaff Fields, and in a short time Cathedral Road, Cowbridge Road East and adjoining streets were flooded to the depth of several feet. Spectators and animals had to be rescued from a circus top in Sophia Gardens. The monkeys were taken to Stone's undertakers in Cowbridge Road East and, imitating the television advertisement of the time, were served with tea and cakes in the funeral parlour. Camels and horses made their own way to safety and were later rounded up near Penarth Road. Rowing boats were brought from Roath Park Lake to rescue people from shops in Cowbridge Road East. Thousands of pounds worth of damage was caused to the National Sports Centre, in Sophia Gardens, while hundreds of houses, offices, shops and scores of cars were affected by floodwater. Volunteers went to the scene to help people, including patients at the Lord Ninian Hospital, in Cathedral Road, who were trapped by the rising water. There had been major floods in Cardiff in the 1920s and 1960s, but the 1979 incident was the worst. It prompted the Welsh Water Authority to launch a multi-million-pound flood prevention scheme in the hope that the 'Great Flood' would not be repeated.

1980

First Woman Deacon

Llandaff Cathedral was the scene of a major protest when the Church in Wales ordained its first woman deacon, the Revd Iris Thomas. When Judge Norman Francis, the Chancellor of the Church in Wales, asked if there were any objections to the

pending ordination fourteen people stood up and by prior arrangement their spokesman objected to the proposal to ordain a woman. Judge Francis ruled that the ordination would be legal under an Act passed by the governing body at Lampeter and the ordination went ahead after the objectors staged a walk-out from the packed cathedral. One of the objectors was the Revd Kenneth Gillingham, parish priest of St Mary the Virgin Church in Bute Street, Cardiff. He joined the Church of England, which had not agreed to the ordination of women at that time. Iris Thomas, who became established in a parish in the Rhondda, was too old to be officially ordained when the Church in Wales went a step further and allowed women to be ordained not just as deacons but as priests. However, she was granted the honorary title of priest in recognition of her pioneering work that had caused a minor split in the Anglican Church in Wales.

The unveiling of the Polish War Memorial outside City Hall in 1980.

A Second World War hero who survived the German concentration camps died in Cardiff in May 1980. He was Dr Josef Wienlawa-Klimaszewski who, as an officer in the Polish cavalry, took part in what became known as the last organised cavalry charge in history. Armed with belts of Molotov cocktails, the horsemen charged German battle tanks and achieved considerable success for a number of hours before fighter planes and bombers brought an end to the encounter. Klimaszewski was taken prisoner but escaped and joined the Polish Free Army, which was reformed in Persia by the British 8th Army. He served under FM Bernard Montgomery in North Africa and Italy, and won the Polish equivalent of the Victoria Cross. An expert in international law, he opted to come to Britain in 1941, but like other displaced persons he had to work as a labourer, unloading fish at Cardiff Docks. He eventually became managing director of the building firm DMD, with which he was involved in building the Empire Pool, the South Stand of the National Stadium and the UWIST building in Cathays Park.

The Queen and the Duke of Edinburgh attended the Welsh Rugby Union's centenary match at the National Ground, and Stewart Williams published the first of his thirty books in the Cardiff Yesterday series recording the history of Cardiff. Stewart was also a keen supporter of the first Cardiff Commercial Radio Station, which was launched this year. The new bridge at Llandaff North was opened, after the previous one had been destroyed in the disastrous flood the previous December. The M4 link from Castleton to Coryton was completed, and Ely-born Shakin' Stevens made the pop charts with 'Hot Dog'.

1981

Peace March

Led by Anne Pettitt, thirty-six women, four babies in pushchairs and six men left Cardiff on 27 August 1981 to march to RAF Greenham Common in Berkshire. They were protesting about the American ground-launched nuclear cruise missiles to be deployed there and demanded a debate on TV with government ministers. When this was refused, many of them stayed at Greenham, camping outdoors in all weathers until the year 2000.

❖   ❖   ❖

The outstanding Cardiff-born cartoonist J.C. Walker died in Hertfordshire in October 1981. For forty years his hard-hitting cartoons appeared in the *South Wales Echo* before he retired in 1966. The Italian government put a price on his head for mocking their fascist leader Mussolini, while his work during the Second World War was a great morale-booster proving that the pen can be mightier than the sword.

A farmer and crack Bisley marksman, 'JC', as he was affectionately known, turned down a lucrative job on the *News of the World* in his early days because he did not want to leave his native city of Cardiff.

Cartoonist J.C. Walker, who was also a champion marksman.

J.C. Walker's famous cartoons appeared in the *South Wales Echo* for forty years.

One of the wittiest writers and speakers, author and playwright Gwyn Thomas also died in 1981. His tongue was as sharp as J.C. Walker's pencil.

This was the year that Diana, Princess of Wales was given the Freedom of the City, and when St Fagans won the village cricket trophy at Lords. Debenhams store and the YMCA in The Walk opened; the Plaza Cinema in North Road and the sports stadium in Sloper Road closed and the fruit market moved from Mill Lane to David Street, and then to Barracks Lane.

1982

Papal Visit

More than 200,000 people greeted Pope John Paul II when he presided over a concelebrated mass and a youth service in Cardiff on Wednesday 2 June 1982 – at the end of his five-day visit to Britain.

The Polish-born Pope won the hearts of 150,000 people at Pontcanna Fields when he started the mass in Welsh. He also turned to Welsh near the end of his sermon about the Holy Eucharist when he said: '*Bobl annwyl Cymru. Byddwch ffyddlon i Grist yn*

Pope John Paul II was made a Freeman of Cardiff by the Lord Mayor Phil Dunleavy.

awr. Ef yw eich Gobaith' ('Dear people of Wales. Be faithful to Christ now. He is your hope').

The Holy Father asked the congregation to remember those who had died in the Falklands War, the shadow of which hung over his visit, and also to pray for those who had died in the conflict between Iran and Iraq and in every place where human blood is shed.

The moment the Pope stepped from the helicopter at Blackweir brought great joy to Cardiff, the city that Bishop Langton Fox has described as the most Catholic in Britain; an area where there were only three known Catholics in 1820 but nineteen Catholic parishes 162 years later.

The arrangements for the event virtually turned the papal mass into an all-night vigil. The great crowd had been advised to be in their places before 8 a.m. – two hours before the mass was due to start. Thousands started their pilgrimage to Cardiff the previous evening, and from dawn the massive job of getting more than 4,000 sick, disabled and elderly people to Pontcanna began. They, and the 4,000 voluntary helpers, were carried by special buses and ambulances from every part of South Wales. From 4 a.m. there was a carnival atmosphere throughout Cardiff as visitors arrived by a hundred special trains and as many coaches.

For four hours before the Holy Father arrived, the crowd was entertained with music and community hymns. Some of the music was provided by St Albans Band, world-famous as the band that plays for international matches at the Wales National Stadium rugby ground in Cardiff. More than twenty bishops and thirty priests concelebrated mass with the Holy Father on the 60ft dais. A choir of 900, including representatives of some of the famous male voice and polyphonic choirs in Wales, had been especially formed to sing the mass, composed by Dom Alan Rees, the choirmaster of Belmont Abbey, and David Neville, the choirmaster at St David's Cathedral, in Cardiff. At the offertory the Welsh folkgroup Ar Log ('For Hire') played a selection of traditional music while representatives from various organisations handed gifts to the Holy Father. These included a miner's lamp, a book of Welsh poems, Welsh pottery, Welsh slate, an etching on steel and some weaving.

As the Pope was slowly driven past the various groups at the end of the mass, thousands spontaneously sang 'We'll keep a welcome in the hillside, We'll keep a welcome in the vales; this land you know will still be singing when you come home again to Wales.'

During the lunch break at Cardiff Castle, the Freedom of Cardiff was bestowed on the Pope by the Lord Mayor of the City, Councillor Phil Dunleavy.

After lunch, thousands lined the streets to watch the Holy Father's journey to Ninian Park, the home of Cardiff City Football Club. Thousands of young people from all over Britain were at the ground for the youth service, where the Pope called for the young people of Britain, including the 33,000 at Ninian Park, to launch a crusade of prayer.

The Pope ended his historic six-day visit to Britain tired and triumphant as he gave a final blessing to all, before boarding his plane for Rome: 'To all the people of England, Scotland and Wales, I say God bless you. May He make you instruments of His peace, and may the peace of Christ reign in your hearts and in your homes.' The Holy Father also gave a special blessing in Welsh: '*Bendith Duw Arnoch! Bendith Duw Arnoch*' ('May God's blessing be on you all').

Some of the thousands who greeted Pope John Paul II in June 1982.

It was appropriate that the Pope should give a message in Welsh, as 1982 was also the year that the Welsh-language television station S4C was launched under the first controller, Owen Edwards. The service was a key element in saving the Welsh language, which supporters feared would be lost with English-only television programmes being screened by the BBC and independent channels. It was the courage of Gwynfor Evans, who in 1966 was elected as Plaid Cymru's first MP when he won the Carmarthen seat, that led to the founding of S4C. He went on hunger strike and stirred the Labour Party, especially Cledwyn Hughes, MP, into agreeing to the establishment of a Welsh-language channel.

A Labour government had accepted the principle of equal validity for the Welsh language on 14 December 1965. The announcement was made by the Secretary of State for Wales James Griffiths, MP for Llanelli. He told the House of Commons he wanted to see the language survive but at the same time did not want to see the differences of language disrupting the unity of Wales as it had done in other countries. He said that equal validity meant any act, writing or thing done in Welsh in Wales would have similar legal force as if it had been done in English. But he warned that unfair and antagonistic action to the majority of non-Welsh speakers had to be avoided.

Griffiths made his historic announcement during debate of a report from a committee, headed by Sir David Hughes Parry, set up to examine the status of the Welsh language. Jim Griffiths rejected one of the committee's most controversial suggestions – that the heads of government departments in Wales should all be Welsh speakers.

Welsh-language activists were far from happy with the policy proposed by the Labour government. They believed that it did not go far enough. Overnight English place names were painted out in cities and towns in Wales. Extremists formed a Welsh Free Army, under the leadership of Cayo Evans, explosives were set off, one outside the Temple of Peace in Cardiff and another at Caernarfon when Charles was invested as Prince of Wales there in 1969. In the 1980s a campaign was launched to try and stop English families from buying rural cottages for holiday homes. Many of these were set on fire. The disunity that Jim Griffiths had feared had become a reality.

Despite these setbacks, the Welsh language – known as the 'Language of the Angels' – continued to progress. In addition to the founding of S4C, Welsh-language schools were established throughout Wales and the principle of bilingualism was accepted by local authorities, courts, post offices, banks and supermarkets. The greatest example can be found at the National Assembly for Wales, where members can speak in either language, which is immediatley translated through headphones.

A family for which the song 'Walk Tall' could have been written was the Barry family of Cardiff. In 1982 Steve Barry won the gold medal for the 30-kilometre walk in the Commonwealth Games in Brisbane, Australia, in a time of 2 hours, 10 minutes and 16 seconds. But Steve would have been the first to acknowledge that his father, Dai Barry, was one of the greatest Welsh walkers and all-round sportsmen of all time. Both father and son were members of Roath Harriers.

In 1939 Dai was in the Welsh walking relay teams that won both the Newport to Swansea race and the London to Brighton race. He was Welsh 20-mile champion from 1951 to 1954, and during that period also held the 10-mile, 7-mile and 2-mile track championships. He finished third to world record holder Roland Hardy and second to Olympic record holder H. Caurgaer. When he was 42 he won the Welsh triple crown over distances of two miles, ten miles and twenty miles. But it was not just as a walker that Dai shone. He was an outstanding boxing referee who officiated at 6,000 bouts, including two Empire Games. He also controlled matches involving world champions Howard Winstone, Ken Buchanan and John Stracey.

He played soccer for Cardiff City in 1936 and for Swansea Town in 1942. During the Second World War he also played for the army against the RAF three times. Not satisfied with that, he played rugby for a number of Cardiff district teams. When he wasn't walking in the summer, he played baseball and was a member of the championship-winning Splott Stars and captained Splott US against GKN in front of a record crowd of 12,000 at Sloper Road.

This was also the year the new BUPA hospital opened; the River Taff flood-protection scheme was inaugurated, following the disastrous floods of December 1979, and the roofs of Sophia Gardens Pavilion and the indoor bowls centre at Llanishen collapsed during a blizzard. The Cogan spurway opened and Crosswell's Brewery closed.

1983

Land of Song

As Wales is acknowledged as the Land of Song, it was only fitting that the capital city should introduce a Cardiff Singers of the World competition. The winner of the first biennial event at St David's Hall was Karita Mattila, a soprano from Finland. In 1985 David Malis, a baritone from the USA, was awarded the prize, and two years later it was Italian soprano Valerie Eposito who impressed the judges. The international flavour of the event was underlined in 1989 when Dmitri Hvorostovsky, the Russian baritone, took the honours. This was also the year that the Welsh baritone Bryn Terfel won the inaugural Lieder award. Two years later another Welsh baritone, Neal Davies, won the Lieder prize while the top award went to Australian soprano Lisa Gasteen.

The Singers of the World competition was the first major event to be held at St David's Hall, the national concert hall and conference centre, which was built on The Hayes, Cardiff. The hall was officially opened in 1983 by the Queen Mother, who was no stranger to the city having visited it following the blitz in 1941. For architects Seymour Harris Partnership, designing St David's Hall was a challenge: to provide a major 2,000-seat concert hall in the cramped space available, and to complicate the issue, the building had to be fitted into an existing planned, and partly built, shopping centre. The result was that, in an incredible five years from conception to completion, an impressive 2,000-seat concert hall, with arguably the best acoustics in Europe, was built directly over the St David's Centre shopping arcade. An open day in August 1982 attracted 21,000 people; nine days later came the first public concert, a free open rehearsal by the Polyphonic Choir. By the time the Queen Mother performed the official opening in February 1983, St David's Hall had already transformed the artistic life of the capital city. As Her Majesty said, 'This exciting development will add greatly to the quality of life for the city of Cardiff and the people of the Principality.'

1984

Brighton Bomb Victim

Sir Anthony Berry, MP, a former managing director of the *Western Mail and Echo*, was one of five people killed when the IRA planted a bomb at the Grand Hotel, Brighton, in 1984. The blast tore apart the hotel where Prime Minister Margaret Thatcher and members of her cabinet and leading MPs were staying for the Conservative party conference. The IRA admitted placing a 100lb bomb in the hotel. Part of their statement read: 'Give Ireland peace and there will be no more war.'

Sir Anthony was born in 1925, the son of newspaper magnate James Berry, Viscount Kemsley, whose roots were in Merthyr. Sir Anthony worked as a sub-editor on the *Western Mail* before being elevated to the board. Though he lived at Miskin Manor, Pontyclun, he was MP for Enfield Southgate and held the junior post of Treasurer of the Household in the Thatcher government. Sir Anthony's first wife, Mary, whom he divorced in 1966, was the elder sister of Frances Ruth Burke, who was to become Countess Spencer and mother of Diana, Princess of Wales. Sir Anthony married Sarah Anne Clifford-Turner in 1966.

Throughout its history the Prince of Wales in St Mary Street had served as a theatre, a pub and a cinema. In 1984 it became a discotheque and later it became a pub again. It was well known to rugby fans, especially those attending matches at the newly completed National Ground in Westgate Street.

The good news for children this year was that the City Council banned corporal punishment in primary and comprehensive schools.

1985

The Rommel Connection

The son of FM Erwin Rommel, at one time Hitler's favourite military commander, has strong links with Cardiff. Manfred Rommel, *Oberburgermeister* of the city's twin town of Stuttgart, in Germany, was a regular visitor to Cardiff. In 1985 Manfred sealed the friendship by presenting the Stuttgart Panels which are displayed at St David's Hall. FM Rommel had commanded a panzer division in France and later led the German Africa Corps against FM Bernard Montgomery's Desert Rats. But Erwin Rommel fell out with the Nazis and was forced to commit suicide in 1944. The events leading up to this were witnessed by his then 15-year-old son Manfred, who was to become a good friend of Cardiff.

There was a triumphant greeting for Cardinal Jozef Glemp, the Primate of Poland, when he visited Cardiff on St David's Day 1985. The visit coincided with the third anniversary of the first aid relief transport from Wales to Poland. The Polish exiles were generous to the folks at home, and an organisation was formed in Cardiff to send aid to the needy people of Poland. Key figures in this venture were the late Vidol and Joan Kuczys, of Kings Road, Canton.

One of the finest youth and community leaders in Cardiff, Albert Bridle, died suddenly while walking in the Castle grounds in the spring of 1985. The pantomimes and concerts he staged were known as Bridle Productions and will long be remembered. It came as no surprise when he gave up his career as an executive with Evan Roberts Store in Cardiff to become a full-time youth leader and later a community leader in the city. Every year from 1948 he sacrificed his Christmas lunch at home to supervise a team of volunteers who fed and entertained about a hundred old or disabled people who would otherwise have spent a lonely Christmas in their own homes.

The Cardiff-based Reardon Smith Shipping Company was wound up in 1985, the year that a heliport opened at East Moors. The Globe Cinema in Albany Road closed, and the Urdd Eisteddfod was held in the city.

1986

On the Buses

The 1985 Transport Act deregulated all bus services, except those in London, and local authorities were told by the Conservative government to establish private 'arm's length' bus companies. In October 1986 Cardiff City and County Council established its own company – Cardiff City Transport Services Limited (trading as Cardiff Bus). This was the biggest change in public transport in the city since electrically-operated trams were introduced in 1902, replacing horse-drawn buses which had operated in the area since the 1840s. The Council owns all the shares in Cardiff Bus and is represented on the board of directors. As a private company, Cardiff Bus is not permitted to receive subsidies and is expected to make a profit for the Council by being run along commercial lines. In 1992, following the closure of the long-established National Welsh Bus Company, Cardiff Bus extended its network of services into Barry and the rural Vale and increased bus services in the Caerphilly area. Each weekday around 80,000 passengers are carried by Cardiff Bus, including pensioners who have been issued with free passes by the National Assembly.

When Wales beat Tonga 15–7 at the Teufaiva Stadium in June 1986, Cardiff-born Glen Webbe, who came on as substitute, became the first Black player to be awarded a Welsh cap. While Glen became a long-serving member of Bridgend, five of the Welsh team who played against Tonga, wing Adrian Hadley, fly-half Jonathan Davies, centre John Devereux, flanker Paul Moriarty and prop Stuart Evans, turned to Rugby League. Back in Cardiff there was a special union fixture when the British Lions lost 15–7 to a Rest of the World XV. The match was to celebrate the International Rugby Board's centenary.

Cardiff-born John Arthur Simpson, an old boy of Cathays High School, Cardiff, was appointed Dean of Canterbury Cathedral in 1986 and held the post until he retired in the year 2000. 1986 was also the year that Marments store, which had stood in Queen Street since 1879, closed and the Royal Mail sorting office was transferred from Westgate Street to Penarth Road. The Holiday Inn, later the Marriott Hotel, opened in Mill Lane.

1987

Barrage of Controversy

The first of five parliamentary Cardiff Barrage bills was presented to the Commons in 1987 but was unsuccessful. There was a great deal of opposition to the £200 million scheme aimed at creating a lake to cover the mudflats near where the rivers Taff and Ely enter the Bristol Channel. The 200-hectare freshwater lake, which was eventually created when the barrage was built in the 1990s, became the centrepiece of a vast renewal programme of the Bay, where the eight miles of waterfront attracted government buildings, entertainment centres, restaurants, hotels and housing. The barrage, which turned 400 acres of wasteland into a lake, costs almost £20 million a year to run and is one of the most expensive civil engineering schemes undertaken on the British coastline.

The idea was conceived by Nicholas Edwards when he was Welsh Secretary. He decided that a bold plan was needed to redevelop the 3,000 acres of industrial dereliction, left by the end of the steel industry and the decline of the docks. The opposition came from those who found the mudflats attractive and environmentalists who wanted the site maintained as one of special scientific interest, hosting overwintering birds from northern Europe. So great was the opposition, inside and outside the city, that five different Cardiff Bay Barrage bills were unsuccessfully presented to parliament between 1987 and 1991. Only when the sixth and last one received formal government backing could the scheme go ahead.

Even then, local opposition, especially from people who feared the barrage would cause major flooding and create a health hazard, managed to delay its passage into law for another two years. Under European law, the drowned site of special scientific interest would have to be replaced by a similar site elsewhere, and this was achieved at a cost of £10 million on land at the Usk Estuary, near Newport. The National Assembly was left to pick up the bill for the ecological changes that had to be made and also for the annual running and maintenance cost of the barrage, which was completed in 2001 and is expected to last for 200 years. Critics believe that the regeneration which has taken place in the Bay area, including the new Millennium Centre, shops, restaurants and pubs, could have been achieved without the barrage.

❖   ❖   ❖

The Cardiff Bay Development Corporation was established in 1987 by the Welsh Office, under Secretary of State Nicholas Edwards. The thirteen-strong board was given the task of overseeing the redevelopment of an area of about 1,089 hectares, comprising parts of the City of Cardiff and the Borough of Vale of Glamorgan. The Corporation continued to operate until 1999 when it was wound up to allow the National Assembly to take control of its functions.

The Institute of Welsh Affairs was founded in 1987, as an independent think-tank, to act as a bridge between public policy makers, the academic community, businesses and non-profit organisations. Part of its plan was to commission research, organise seminars, lectures and conferences, facilitate debate, and publish reports and policy papers. Its central aim was to develop practical proposals for policy innovation and improvement. The Cardiff-based organisation has over 1,100 individual members and 150 corporate members.

Since being founded in 1987, Cardiff Cobras has been one of the most successful clubs at any level in the history of British American football, having had only three unsuccessful seasons over seventeen years (it has won 99 games, lost 45 and drawn 3). The team plays at Llanrumney. This was the year that the new City Line railway service was inaugurated, linking Queen Street with Coryton, Radyr, Fairwater, Danescourt and Ninian Park. The statue of Nye Bevan was unveiled in Queen Street, the first pop concert, starring David Bowie, was held at the Arms Park, and the last military tattoo was staged at Cardiff Castle.

1988

Colleges Merge

The merger of the University College, Cardiff and the University of Wales Institute of Science and Technology took place in 1988. The new college, the history of which can be traced back to late Victorian times, is rated excellent throughout the world in mechanical engineering, chemistry, architecture, environmental engineering, marine geography, English language, optometry, philosophy, psychology, city and regional planning, pharmacy, electrical and electronic engineering, archaeology and ancient history, biology, accounting and finance, anatomy and physiology, biochemistry, civil engineering, dentistry, education and medicine. It also offers a range of sports facilities to its 14,000 students.

A Common Cold Centre, involved in clinical trials and basic research on ineffective and allergic diseases of the upper airways, was established at the University Hospital of Wales in 1988. It conducts clinical trials on new treatments for hay fever, the common cold and influenza. The centre also continues the pioneering work into the study of asthma that was launched at St David's Hospital in 1935. Pollen and spore counts have been taken in Cardiff since 1954, and it is thought that this is the longest continuous pollen and spore data set for any site worldwide.

In 1988 the churches of Cardiff were called together by Cardiff Bay Development Corporation to discuss the role of Christianity in Cardiff Bay.

With the Corporation's help, a redundant light vessel that had been used by Trinity House in coastal waters around Britain was purchased and berthed at Cardiff Docks, where it is used as a unique place of worship. The vessel, which was launched at Dartmouth in 1953, has been restored and refurbished by volunteers – welders, metal workers, mechanical engineers, carpenters, electricians and plumbers. Regular services are held on board, where there is also a snack bar. The light vessel had been made redundant as automation was introduced to light beacons. The lighthouse on Flat Holm was also switched to automatic control in 1988.

The former lightship which is now a church berthed at Cardiff Bay.

The Retired and Senior Volunteer Programme started in Cardiff in 1988, and since then has grown steadily spreading to almost every region of the country. RSVP believes that older people have a lifetime of skills and experience which, when brought into volunteering activities, is of immeasurable benefit in their own communities. Through their involvement in community activities, the volunteers themselves receive an enormous benefit in terms of improved health and self-confidence.

The new County Hall was established at Cardiff Bay and the Central Library was transferred from The Hayes to St David's Link. The New Theatre reopened after its first major refurbishment in eighty years, and HTV moved its operation from Pontcanna to Culverhouse Cross. The first ten-pin bowling venue for Wales opened in Newport Road, and Spillers warehouse at Cardiff Bay was converted into flats. Direct flights were inaugurated between Cardiff Wales Airport and Toronto in Canada. The deaths were announced of film director Richard Marquand and composer and conductor Arwel Hughes.

1989

Colin the Great

Colin Jackson is not only the greatest athlete to be born in Cardiff but ranks as one of the best track performers in the world. In 1988 he won a silver medal for the 110-metre hurdles at the Seoul Olympics. In 1989 he struck silver in the 110-metre hurdles in the World Cup competition, finished first in the 1992 event and second in 1998. He was World Champion over the distance in 1993 and 1999 and European Champion in 1994, 1998 and 2002. He took the gold medal in the Commonwealth Games in 1990 and 1994 and finished first in the European Cup tournament in 1989 and 1998. In addition he won fourteen senior Welsh titles, ten British outdoor and six indoor titles and world records for the 100-metres outdoors and 60-metres indoors. Although he competed in three Olympic Games, he never acheieved a gold medal. He was awarded the MBE in 1990.

Wheelchair rugby was introduced to the city when Keith Jones ignored his handicap and formed the Cardiff Pirates in 1989. He captained the team and became chairman of the Welsh Wheelchair Rugby Association. His greatest moment was when he represented Great Britain at the Paralympics in Sydney in 2000.

The Hanafi mosque, in Broadway, the largest mosque in Wales at that time, was destroyed by fire in 1989. In 2005, as Cardiff celebrated its 100th anniversary as a city, plans were well advanced to build a new mosque in Woodville Road. This will be one of ten mosques catering for thousands of Muslims who live in the capital. The building in Woodville Road will be only the third purpose-built mosque in Cardiff, most of the others being created from converting churches or warehouses. The other two purpose-built mosques are in Alice Street and Moira Street.

The first Muslims to arrive in Cardiff were seamen from the Yemen. Their imam – spiritual leader – was Sheik Hassan Ismail, who was succeeded by his foster-son Sheik Said Hassan, who worked as a welder in Cardiff before taking over as the imam, a post he had held for forty-nine years by 2005. Scores of Muslim seamen from Cardiff were killed on active duty with the Merchant Navy during the Second World War.

Many immigrants from the Punjab made their home in Cardiff, and a Sikh temple was established in Tudor Street in 1989 to serve their spiritual and social needs.

There are two gurdwaras – Sikh temples – in Cardiff and the Sikh Association of South Wales has about a hundred members. On big occasions about 250 people from all over Wales and England join the Sikh community in Cardiff. Sikhism is the youngest of the world religions, barely 500 years old, and was founded by Guru Nanak at a time when India was being torn apart by castes, sectarianism, religious factions and fanaticism. There are now about 20 million Sikhs worldwide, mostly living in the Sikh homeland of the Punjab. Britain is home to about 750,000 devotees – the largest community of Sikhs outside India.

Local Sikhs were at the Arms Park in 1958 when one of their heroes, Indian Milkha Singh won gold in the 400 metres at the Empire Games. Milkha, known as the 'Flying Sikh', is acknowledged as the greatest athlete to hail from his part of the world.

❖   ❖   ❖

Hindu worshippers started to arrive in Britain during the late '50s and early '60s, and a number of them settled in Cardiff, bringing with them their culture, their traditions, their heritage and above all their religion. In 1989 they staged an exhibition, opened by Alun Michael, MP, marking the tenth anniversary of the establishment of a temple in a disused synagogue. The temple gradually became too small to accommodate the worshippers so a new property in Merches Gardens, Grangetown was bought for £150,000 and renovation of the two-storey property started. Work was undertaken by many members during their spare time, holidays and weekends with youngsters taking the opportunity to acquire manual skills such as carpentry, electrical wiring, building and plumbing. The women and girls also took part in building the Shree Swaminarayan temple.

The building was opened on 25 September 1993, when His Holiness Acharya Maharaj Shree Tejendraprasadji Maharaj and Her Holiness Gadiwala came to the city to celebrate the occasion. On the same day a procession took place through the centre of Cardiff. Followers from all over the UK, India, USA and Africa joined in the festivities.

❖   ❖   ❖

This was the year that Britain's first Japanese Studies Centre opened at the University in Cardiff and Ffilm Cymru was established in the city. A Welsh Hall of Fame was set up at the County Hall, but later transferred to the Folk Museum at St Fagans. An athletics stadium was established at Leckwith; an extension to the BUPA hospital was opened; a warehouse was converted into the Celtic Hotel; and the Central Link Road was inaugurated. *Wales on Sunday* was launched, the first Sunday newspaper to be published in Cardiff since the *Empire News* closed in the early 1960s.

1990

Saddam's Hostage

Oil-pipe manager Patrick Trigg was the last British hostage to leave Iraq before the Gulf War started in 1991. He was allowed to leave Saddam Hussain's jail just seven days earlier after being cleared of trying to escape illegally from the country where he had worked for nearly nine years. The Cardiff-born 54-year-old was taken to a secret prison and placed in solitary confinement on 3 September 1990. As he walked around his cell measuring four paces by two, Patrick decided that prayer was the best antidote for the loneliness, despair and isolation he faced. He fell back on the hymns and prayers that he remembered from when he and his twin brother, Theodore, had been altar boys at St Mary of the Angels Church, Canton. He knotted a blanket thread to use as a rosary, but this was confiscated by the guards. Patrick slept on the stone floor of his red-walled cell, lit twenty-four hours a day by a television monitor. His food, either lentil soup or cabbage water, was shoved through a letterbox hatch twice a day. His only respite was when he was taken from the cell for questioning. He spent Christmas Day alone in his cell, but on Boxing Day he was taken to an administration office where there was a Madeira cake, made by the wife of his interrogator, with a number of candles on it. He was told it was for his birthday, and he had to explain that Christmas was the birthday of Christ. He held hands with the Muslim officers and they all sang 'Happy Birthday' to Jesus!

In January 1991 Patrick was found not guilty by the court and was allowed to leave for Britain. There was great joy at St Paul's Church in Cardiff when Patrick attended mass, celebrated by Canon Tom Dunne. It was an occasion when the Sign of Peace had truly great significance.

The most successful Welsh diver, Cardiff-born Robert Morgan, won the gold medal for the 10-metre highboard (platform) event at the Commonwealth Games in New Zealand in 1990 logging a score of 639.84. Four years earlier Robert took the bronze medal at the Commonwealth Games in Edinburgh with a score of 561.54.

Cardiff Bay Channel Fleet was formed in 1990, when a group of enthusiastic racing sailors, from Cardiff Yacht Club, Penarth Yacht Club and Penarth Motor Boat and Sail Club, decided that yacht racing within the Cardiff Bay area needed to be organised on a firm basis. For the first time a race programme was published, with capable race officers recruited from within the racing fleet rather than from the three yacht clubs. In 1992 a permanent race officer was appointed whose responsibility it was to run the actual racing, promulgate the results and maintain yacht handicap records.

Mary Anne Street was Cardiff's biggest slum in the nineteenth century, with up to fifty-seven people living in a two-roomed, windowless terraced house. Cholera was rife in the street, which was home to refugees from the Great Irish Famine. In 1990 the Irish connection was renewed when Jurys Hotel, owned by a company from Ireland, opened on the cleared side of the street. This was also the year that the new magistrates' court opened in Fitzalan Place, the Capitol Shopping Centre was established and The Tube, an information office for visitors, started serving Cardiff Bay. Cardiff Arms Park, scene of so many memorable rugby matches, staged one of its most popular concerts when the Rolling Stones played to a full house.

Two of Cardiff's finest boxers, Jack Petersen and Joe Erskine, died in 1990, and some of the top names in the sport attended their funerals in Cardiff. Welsh international fullback Alf Sherwood, a stalwart of Cardiff City's postwar era, also died.

1991

Ely Riots

Riots broke out in the Ely area of Cardiff in 1991 after a row over which shop should sell bread. The incidents, during which a shopkeeper suffered racial abuse, highlighted the problems of unemployment and deeper social issues in the area. Ironically, Ely has one of the lowest ethnic minority populations in Cardiff. The disturbances were centred around Wilson Road, and a lot of local residents only knew there was anything going on by the press reports and the noisy police helicopter with its searchlight keeping them awake at night. The majority of Ely people are decent and hard-working, and it was their protests against the troublemakers that helped to calm the situation.

The best women's rugby teams gathered in Cardiff in 1991 for the first Women's World Rugby Championship. There was a great deal of support for the tournament, even from the purists who saw it as a man's game. The decision to hold the Cardiff event, which did not have the official backing of the International Rugby Board, was taken after a successful tournament in New Zealand in 1990. Twelve teams took part at Cardiff, when the United States beat England 19–6 in the final.

A family living in Canton celebrated Christmas every day of the year – until they sold their amazing collection of Nativity cribs to a Japanese company. Their treasure chest of Christmas items, including more than 400 Nativity sets, was amassed by Count Andrew Hubert von Staufer and his wife, Maria, whose terraced home was appropriately named Wassail House. The von Staufers built up the collection with items from nearly every corner of the world. Part of the multi-thousand pounds deal they made with the Japanese company was for their daughter to spend time working in their factory where they planned to make and sell replicas of the cribs.

1992

The Main Event

One of the biggest boxing matches to be staged in Cardiff was when Lennox Lewis fought Frank Bruno for the WBA heavyweight championship in 1992. The fight was held at the National Ground, and although Lewis was favourite to retain his title there was a great deal of support for Bruno. Lewis won on a technical knockout in the seventh round. The after-fight celebrations at the Jackson Hall, in Westgate Street, was attended by celebrities from many walks of life and was voted one of the best parties ever held in the city.

Another major event held at the National Ground that year was the male voice choir concert of 10,000 voices. Choirs from all parts of Wales took part in the show, in the appropriate setting of a rugby ground that had echoed with hymns and arias through the generations.

❖   ❖   ❖

An outstanding landmark at Cardiff Bay is the Norwegian church, which was moved from its original site near the docks gate to a location overlooking the harbour. The church, which was dedicated in 1868, was built to serve the hundreds of Norwegian seamen whose ships were bringing pit props to Cardiff and returning with holds full of coal. Until 1915 it was a spiritual link for up to 73,000 Scandinavian merchant men. Before it closed in 1974 it was the oldest surviving Norwegian church in Britain. The best-selling author Roald Dahl was born in Cardiff of Norwegian parents and was baptised at the church. In the 1980s, when the Norwegian Church Preservation Trust was established to salvage the derelict church, Dahl became its first president, but he died on 23 November 1990, before the reconstruction of the building was complete. The Preservation Trust, together with a support group in Bergen in Norway, raised £250,000 to dismantle the church and re-erect it on

In 1987 Cardiff's Norwegian church was dismantled and moved from its original site in Bute West Dock into storage. It was eventually rebuilt and reopened in 1992 in Britannia Park as an arts centre.

its new site. It no longer serves as a church but hosts exhibitions and concerts and caters for hungry visitors to the Bay.

❖   ❖   ❖

The Welsh School of Medicine, in Cardiff, has always been in the front line of new developments, and this was underlined in 1992 when the Welsh Heart Research Unit opened at the University Hospital of Wales. The unit was linked to the name of opera singer Sir Geraint Evans who had suffered heart problems himself. The first centre in Britain for sports science and sports medicine opened at the National Sports Centre in Sophia Gardens in 1992. This was also the year that the first multi-screen cinema opened at The Odeon, Queen Street.

1993

World Champion

The year 1993 was a golden year for Cardiff boxers, especially Steve Robinson who was crowned World Featherweight Champion in circumstances unique in the sport. Steve, the Ely man who had won only thirteen of his twenty-three professional fights, was given just two days' notice for the world-title fight against Englishman John Davison. Steve was roped in as a late substitute after the reigning world champion, Ruben Palacios of Columbia, failed an HIV test and was stripped of his title. Against all the odds, the Cardiff man won on points and became the first boxer from the city to hold a world title. He proved a worthy wearer of the World Belt, which he successfully defended seven times in thirty months, before being knocked out in the eighth round by Prince Naseem Hamed in 1995.

But Steve, dubbed by boxing writers as the 'Cinderella Man', was not finished. In December 1999 he beat John Jo Irwin to win the European featherweight championship only to lose it the following June when Istvan Kovacs beat him on points. Steve hung up his gloves in 2002 after losing six bouts in succession. He will always be remembered as the super sub who won the hearts of boxing fans, not only for his skill in the ring but also for the dignity with which he conducted himself.

Jimmy Thomas, who was awarded the MBE for his work for young people in Cardiff and his service as a magistrate in the juvenile court, was ordained a Catholic priest in 1993. He was based in St Teilo's parish, Whitchurch, before being appointed parish priest of St David's, Bettws, Newport.

1994

Forensic Expert

As a Home Office pathologist, Professor Bernard Knight attended the scenes of many murders, but none so gruesome as the mass murders at a house in Cromwell Street, Gloucester, in 1994. Fred and Rosemary West were accused of killing ten women, some of whose remains were found buried in the house and garden. Professor Knight, who was born in Paget Street, Cardiff, in 1931, was puzzled to find that either a finger or toe was missing from all the bodies, which suggested to some people that the killings had taken place as part of a ritual. Fred West hanged himself in a prison cell in 1995. His wife was given a life sentence.

Bernard moved from Grangetown to Fairwater as a youngster and attended Herbert Thomson School and St Illtyd's College. His family moved to Swansea, and for a while he worked on a farm on the Gower. He won a scholarship and started work as laboratory technician in the Cardiff Royal Infirmary in 1948. Bernard joined the army as a regular in 1956 and was posted to Malaya during the terrorist emergency. When he left the army in 1959, he went to work in forensic pathology and returned home to lecture in the subject at Cardiff Royal Infirmary. This was the first of a number of similar posts that led to him being elected President of the British Association in Forensic Medicine, the Forensic Science Society and Vice-President of the International Academy of Legal Medicine. He was awarded the CBE in 1993, for services to forensic medicine.

Bernard put his knowledge of forensic medicine to good use by writing nine best-selling crime novels. As Cardiff celebrated its 100th anniversary, he was working on the tenth of his Crowner John mysteries, based on a twelfth-century coroner. The first of these books was dramatised by the BBC in March 2005.

❖   ❖   ❖

This was the year when work started on constructing the Cardiff Barrage and when the link between Pentwyn and the M4 was completed. The *Celtic Challenger*, the last ocean-going vessel registered in Cardiff, made its maiden voyage around the time that the former Merchant Navy Club, later the Station Hotel, was demolished. A memorial plaque to Dic Penderyn (Richard Lewis) was placed at the St Mary's Street end of Cardiff Market, near the spot where he was hanged in 1831, following the Merthyr riots. Another boy from the Valleys, singer Tom Jones was made a Fellow of the Welsh College of Music and Drama in 1994, the year that the *South Wales Echo* became a tabloid newspaper. Spillers, on the Hayes, believed to be one of the oldest record shops in the world, celebrated its centenary in 1994; it started selling sheet music in 1894. The Sir Julian Hodge Centre was opened, run by the Wallich Clifford

Sir Julian Hodge (left) and Viscount Tonypandy officially opened the Sir Julian Hodge Centre in Broadway, Roath, on 24 March 1994.

Community, a charity which provides accommodation for the homeless. Colin Jackson set a new world record for the 60-metres hurdles, and Gus Risman, one of the greatest Rugby League players of all time, died on 17 October.

1995

The People's Lord Mayor

Irishman Ricky Ormond was acclaimed as the 'People's Lord Mayor' during his year of office in 1994/5. His installation was thrown open to young and old people of all walks of life, and not confined to the good and great. When he was asked to see off a mercy convoy to war-torn Croatia he opted to go on the journey as a helper.

Lord Mayor Ricky Ormonde, Lady Mayoress Valerie Swinburn and Fr Bernard Whithouse.

A highlight of his year was when he presented the Freedom of the City to the South Wales miners who for more than a century had made Cardiff the greatest coal-exporting port in the world. Ricky died in March 2004, after losing his battle against cancer, during which he was cared for by his devoted wife, Valerie, who had been Lady Mayoress during his year of office.

They are controversial, they harmonise and they are a regular part of the Cardiff scene: Cor Cochion Caerdydd, also known as the Red Choir, can be seen most Saturdays outside the back of Cardiff Library. Since they were formed in 1983, the choir, campaigning for peace, justice and freedom, has raised thousands of pounds for a variety of charities. Between 1995 and 1998 they raised hundreds of pounds for the families of striking Liverpool dockers. The choir also formed singing pickets outside the gates of Cardiff Docks to protest at cargoes being diverted from Liverpool to the Welsh port. The dockers was just one of the many causes taken up by the choir, who sang on the front line in Northern Ireland and Palestine, and whose battle against apartheid in South Africa became legendary. The choir has adopted 'Askatali' – 'Children of Africa' – as their own anthem. They greeted a delighted Archbishop Tutu with it when he visited South Wales.

Two-ton Tessie O'Shea, Cardiff-born entertainer, died in Florida, where she had lived for many years. The deaths also took place of actress Rachel Thomas, author and critic Glyn Jones and Dr Dilwyn John, former curator of the National Museum of Wales. This was also the year that the Bute Tunnel and Taff Viaduct was opened by EU Commissioner Neil Kinnock and when the new retractable road bridge at Queen Alexandra Docks was completed. Littlewoods Pools closed their Cardiff office, the continental-style Café Quarter started operating in Mill Lane, Harry Ramsden's fish and chip restaurant came to the Bay and Techniquest was established in neighbouring premises. A mural of the docks was unveiled in Stuart Street, the Welsh National Tennis Centre was launched in Ocean Way and construction started on the Nippon Electric Glass Company's factory at East Moors. Shirley Bassey sang at Cardiff Castle, and the Italian tenor Luciano Pavarotti starred at the CIA in a concert to raise money for Ty Hafan Children's Home, and the Welsh National Opera Company staged a free concert in front of the City Hall.

1996

Leader of the Band

The man who played more times at Cardiff rugby grounds than any international player died in 1996, at the age of eighty-two. John Williams was not a rugby player but

the much-loved leader of St Alban's Band, with which he played or led for sixty years before he retired in 1987. John not only led the band but the mass choir of fans, especially those on the famous North Bank. Opposing teams said the band and the singing fans were worth ten points to Wales or Cardiff. John and the band also led the annual Corpus Christi processions, when up to 10,000 Catholic children attended benediction or mass in Cardiff Castle grounds, the Arms Park, or the National Stadium. His biggest problem over six decades was drowning out the noise of the peacocks at the castle!

Band leader John Williams, his son and grandson – members of St Alban's Band.

Another great man, rugby international Clem Thomas, died in 1996. He was also a highly respected sports writer.

Parishioners celebrated the 125th anniversary of St David's Church, Ely, during the weekend of 23 and 24 November 1996. Among those taking part were the Archbishop of Wales, the Most Revd Alwyn Rice Jones, Bishop Roy Davies, of Llandaff, and Viscount Tonypandy. The service was also a fitting silver jubilee tribute to the Revd Jack Buttimore, who had been parish priest for twenty-five years. The church had been consecrated by Bishop Ollivant on 23 November 1871.

A local government reorganisation in 1996 extended Cardiff's boundary to include Creigiau, Pentyrch and Gwaelod-y-Garth. It was also the year that the Celtic Gateway Business Park at Cardiff Bay opened and when the *Western Mail*, *South Wales Echo*, *Wales on Sunday* and Celtic Press were sold to Trinity Holdings, owners of the *Daily Mirror*.

1997

'Yes' to Assembly

Tony Blair's New Labour government was elected to run Britain in May 1997 and soon afterwards published proposals for a parliament for Scotland and an assembly for Wales. Scotland voted overwhelmingly in favour of such a move, but there was a great deal of apathy in Wales, where only just over 50 per cent of the electorate bothered to vote on 18 September 1997. The result was very close with the assembly being approved by less than 7,000 votes, with electors in Cardiff opposing it decisively. The 'no' camp, headed by Robert Hodge, the son of Sir Julian Hodge, was in the lead until the very last result, that of Carmarthen, was declared. The 'yes' vote there was huge, which is not surprising for this was the constituency which had returned Gwynfor Evans, the first Plaid Cymru MP, to parliament in a 1966 by-election. Despite Cardiff's opposition to an assembly the capital was chosen for the new governing body, which Labour, after the first elections in May 1998, controlled by a small majority and later had to form a coalition with the Liberal Democrats to continue in power. In the first five years the assembly had three different First Ministers, former Secretary of State for Wales Ron Davies, MP for Caerphilly, followed by two men who had served Cardiff as MPs, Alun Michael and Rhodri Morgan.

The first major row was over where the assembly would sit. There was disappointment when the City Hall was rejected in favour of a temporary home to be followed by a purpose-built headquarters in Cardiff Bay, which was beginning to develop as a major residential, entertainment and business centre. The Welsh National Opera Company staged a free open-air concert there in July 1997, and a Hollywood Bowl-style 26-lane ten-pin bowling alley opened at the Bay in August, the same month as the Bay's Retail Park was launched. A twelve-screen UCI cinema showed its first films two months later.

The 1997 referendum was not the first time that Wales had been given the chance of having a form of government outside Westminster. On St David's Day 1979, electors in Wales soundly defeated proposals put forward by the Labour government led by James Callaghan, MP for Cardiff South-east.

The tragic death of the Princess of Wales on 31 August 1997, following a car crash in Paris, caused great grief in Cardiff, a city she loved and often visited. She watched international rugby matches and supported local charities, especially Ty Hafan, the organisation that built a home for terminally ill children in the grounds of Sully Hospital. The city and the nation came to a standstill at noon on Saturday 6 September, as a minute's silence was observed to mark the start of the funeral service at Westminster Cathedral, London.

Former pupils of St Cadoc's, Llanrumney, had a double reason to mourn. Mother Teresa, the saintly nun who had visited their school in 1967, died on the day before Diana's funeral. A third death to affect the city was that of Viscount Tonypandy, the former George Thomas, who had represented Cardiff West in the House of Commons since 1945 and who had held high office, including Secretary of State for Wales and Speaker of the Commons. Sir Lincoln Hallinan, a former Cardiff Conservative Alderman and stipendiary magistrate, died in West Wales. In one general election he had unsuccessfully opposed George Thomas in Cardiff West. The sports journalist with the best known byline in Wales, J.B.G. Thomas, also died in 1997. He was an outstanding rugby reporter.

President Mary Robinson of Ireland came to Cardiff on 2 February 1997 and was in a cheerful mood after watching her country's rugby union team beat Wales at the National Stadium. After attending mass at St David's Cathedral she hosted a reception at Cardiff Castle and greeted scores of Irish exiles who had settled in the city. She thanked the city for welcoming Irish people, especially the refugees of the Great Famine of the 1840s, who had adopted Cardiff as their home. She congratulated Irish dance champion Peter Harding of Llanishen, Cardiff, who a few days earlier had successfully auditioned for the world-famous Riverdance Company.

❖   ❖   ❖

More than twenty Catholic priests, all old boys of St Illtyd's College, concelebrated a special mass to mark the De La Salle teaching order's seventy-five years in the city (right). The service, at St Alban's Church, marked the end of the De La Salle brothers' links with the city, which started when they opened St Illtyd's College, the first Catholic grammar school in Wales, in 1922.

❖   ❖   ❖

This was the year that Tony Blair laid the foundation stone for the Millennium Stadium and the demolition of the former National Ground was started. The statue of boxer 'Peerless' Jim Driscoll was unveiled near the site of the demolished Central Boys Club where he used to train. The Cardiff Devils won their first Superleague title, Brains Brewery took over Crown Buckley Brewery in Pontyclun and the ROF factory at Llanishen closed.

1998

European Summit

Leaders of all the European Union countries met in Cardiff for a European summit in 1998, at which a comprehensive Sustainable Development Strategy was agreed. This meant that environmental considerations would be integrated into all EU policy areas as a first step towards sustainable development. Critics, including Plaid Cymru MEP Jill Evans, were disappointed when the resolution which had been agreed in Cardiff was not endorsed at the next EU summit in Göteborg.

The Cardiff summit resulted in the biggest gathering of top political figures ever to come to Cardiff. They were greeted on the eve of the summit by 4,000 farmers and

Crowds lobbied for justice for the Third World when the European Summit took place in Cardiff in 1998.

countryside campaigners who were pressing for an early end to the ban on British beef exports and for more support for rural areas hit by unemployment in the agricultural industry. They marched to the City Hall after holding a rally at the Arms Park. They also handed a petition, which laid out their fears for the loss of 8,000 farming jobs in Britain, to the Welsh Office. As well as farmers, members of the Women's Institute, livestock auctioneers, vets and agricultural sales workers were represented to demonstrate the depth of the crisis. Politicians critical of the EU, including former Conservative chairman Lord Tebbit and former Tory Chancellor Norman Lamont, also met in Cardiff under the banner of the Anti-Maastricht Alliance.

The European leaders were upstaged by the South African president Nelson Mandela, who was a guest of honour at the summit. The man who had brought an end to apartheid in his homeland was given the Freedom of Cardiff in an impressive ceremony at Cardiff Castle. He was also cheered when he went walkabout in Park Place. There was a special link between Mandela and South Wales where the anti-apartheid movement was always strong. A month before the summit the Emperor and Empress of Japan paid a visit to Cardiff.

South African President Nelson Mandela at Cardiff Castle, 1998.

Singer Charlotte Church rocketed to international fame at the age of 12, when she was still a pupil at Bishop of Llandaff School, Cardiff. The girl with the platinum voice was born in Llandaff on 21 February 1986 and was discovered after being persuaded to sing when she introduced her aunt on a television talent show. Charlotte's debut album, *Voice of an Angel*, released in 1998, stunned the music world and her 2000 Christmas collection *Dream a Dream* won a platinum award in America. She was named as one of the top ten female vocalists worldwide in 2000 with Madonna and Janet Jackson were among the other singers listed by Billboard. By the time she was 18, Charlotte had sold more than 10 million records and was one of the youngest millionaires in Britain. She continued to live in Cardiff, remained close to her family and school friends and attracted a great deal of attention from the press. Yet she stayed in the background when she attended a social evening to say goodbye to the John of God Sisters who had taught her when she was a pupil at St Mary's Primary School, Canton.

In 1998 Paddy Irish, who had starred in Ely and Grangetown baseball teams, died in Wexford, Ireland. He also played rugby for Pontypool and was an international marksman for Ireland. He had a secret – he was in reality Catholic priest Fr Dermot Clancy, who played under the alias of Paddy Irish so he would not upset Archbishop John Murphy.

❖   ❖   ❖

This was the year that a memorial was unveiled at Llandaff Cathedral to Welsh Regiment members who were killed in the Korean War in the 1950s. The Wales Empire Pool, built for the Games in 1958, was closed and demolished to make way for the Millennium Stadium; the Welsh Industrial and Maritime Museum was also closed. New developments included the Village Hotel at Coryton and the Holiday Inn Express at Atlantic Wharf. The city's second Welsh-language comprehensive school was established at the former Waterhall School in Plasmawr. The Welsh International film festival was held in Cardiff for the first time after being staged at Aberystwyth for nine years. Red Dragon Radio was sold to Capital Radio and 24-hour shopping was introduced by Tesco at their store in Western Avenue.

1999

National Assembly Opened

There was pomp and ceremony at Cardiff Bay on 26 May 1999, when Her Majesty the Queen, accompanied by the Prince of Wales, opened the first session of the National Assembly for Wales in its temporary headquarters.

During the ceremony, the Queen signed a document on which was written the opening words of the Government of Wales Act.

The assembly has sixty members, including the Presiding Officer, the role of which was held from day one by former Plaid Cymru MP Lord Dafydd Ellis Thomas. The assembly can introduce only secondary legislation, covering areas including legislation, health, training, environment, housing, tourism and agriculture. It has no powers to alter income tax, but it does allocate the funds made available to Wales from the Treasury of the UK. Wales remains within the framework of the United Kingdom, and laws passed by parliament at Westminster still apply to Wales. As Cardiff celebrated its 100th anniversary, all politicians were considering the future of the assembly; some wanted it to be given more power and others doubted whether it should continue. The arguments are likely to go on for a long time to come.

Rhodri Morgan, the third person to be elected First Minister of the National Assembly of Wales.

It was fitting that the Millennium Stadium should be christened with the greatest event to be held in Cardiff since the Empire Games in 1958. The Rugby Union World Cup in 1999 was the curtain-raiser for many prestigious events held at the stadium acclaimed as one of the finest in the world. It was built at a cost of £120 million, with the Welsh Rugby Union meeting 60 per cent of the cost and the balance being funded by the National Lottery. With seating for more than 70,000 spectators and a retractable roof, the stadium was a worthy successor to the National Ground and the Arms Park where rugby internationals had been played in the past. Preliminary rounds for the World Cup were played, not only in Wales but in England, Scotland and France. The first game in Cardiff took place on Friday 1 October and saw Wales beat Argentina by 23 points to 18. Wales reached the quarter-finals, only to lose 24–9 to Australia who went on to win the World Cup by beating France 35–12. Both this game and the play-off for the third place, in which South Africa beat new Zealand 22–18, were played in front of full houses at the Millennium Stadium. Over the next few years the stadium hosted FA Cup finals, Football League finals and Rugby League finals, as well as soccer and rugby internationals.

It is said that if everyone in Cardiff gave blood a large percentage of it would be green. Thousands of Irish people came to the old town after fleeing the Great Famine in Ireland in the 1840s. They helped to build the docks and railways, and the 1881 Census revealed there were seventy-one Irish areas in Cardiff. In 1999 the Wales Famine Forum, at the instigation of students of Irish-language classes in the city, established a memorial to victims of the Irish Famine and all Irish people who have lived in Wales. The Celtic cross, donated by Mossford Monumental Masons, can be seen in Cathays Cemetery, near the site of the demolished Catholic chapel, some of the bricks from which were used for the plinth. The inscriptions are in English, Welsh, Irish and Latin. The ancestors of the chairman of the forum, John Sweeney, were among those who came to Cardiff after the famine. Secretary Barry Tobin, who was born in Cork, was the Irish-language teacher when the idea for the memorial was suggested.

Cathays Cemetery is a fitting location for the memorial as buried in a mass unmarked grave, adjacent to Wedal Road, are 349 Irish people who died of cholera in the 1850s. Also buried in this patch are the bodies which were exhumed from the Presbyterian church graveyard when the St David Centre was developed in the 1960s. The Famine Forum organises services of reflection at the memorial every St Patrick's Day.

A couple who were brought together by their mutual love of music celebrated their diamond wedding anniversary in 1999. George and Gwyneth Nibblet, of Bwlch Road, Fairwater, Cardiff, were married at Risca on 8 April 1939, after meeting for the first time when they were both violinists with the Risca Orchestral Society. They moved to Cardiff when they returned from honeymoon. Sadly Gwyneth died just twelve days after the diamond celebrations. In his 85th year George was still accompanist to the Cardiff Police Choir and during his life he had been the conductor or accompanist for various male voice choirs and was connected with the Cardiff Male Voice Choir for many years. One of his proudest moments was when he led the choir at a Festival of Remembrance at the Colston Hall, Bristol.

This was the year that the first games were played at the Millennium Stadium and when the stadium roof opened and closed for the first time. The Cardiff Barrage was completed, and the first sailing competion took place on the lake that was created. The Sir Geraint Evans Heart Research Centre was opened at the University Hospital of Wales, and the Accident and Emergency department was transferred to UHW from Cardiff Royal Infirmary. The Ty Hafan Centre for critically ill children was opened in the grounds of Sully Hospital. A centre for visual arts was established at the Old Library in The Hayes at a time when the former Prince of Wales Theatre was converted into a pub. The ABC cinema in Queen Street closed, but the Globe Cinema in Albany Road was given a new lease of life by Chapter Arts. Cardiff Devils ice hockey team won the Super League title for the second time, and Simply Red performed at an open-air concert at Cardiff Castle.

2000

From Crèche to Cabinet

At the dawn of the new millennium, the Welsh Office in Cardiff was headed by Paul Murphy and Don Toughig, two men of Gwent who had known each other since being together in nursery school and then St Francis Primary School, Abersychan.

Paul was Secretary of State for Wales, and Don was Minister of State for Wales. Paul had previously been Minister of State in troubled Northern Ireland and had played a major role in the talks leading up to the Good Friday Agreement. When Republicans started speaking in Irish at one meeting, Paul took the heat out of the occasion by replying in Welsh. He was later to return to Northern Ireland as Secretary of State.

Don Toughig made one of the most remarkable comebacks in political history when he was elected to succeed

The two little boys at a nursery school at Abercarn became two of the most powerful men in Wales. Wearing a hat is Paul Murphy, a future Secretary of State for Wales and the other lad is Don Toughig, a future Minister of State at the Welsh Office.

former Labour leader Neil Kinnock as MP for Islwyn, for the victory came four years after he had been punished by the Labour Party for daring to oppose its plans to close St Albans Comprehensive School at Pontypool. The ruling Labour group on Gwent County Council took the whip away from him for three months and sacked him from the powerful position of vice-chairman of the county finance committee. To add salt to Labour's wounds the then Conservative Secretary of State for Wales, David Hunt, refused to approve the closure of the school.

The need for forgiveness was emphasised by Archbishop Desmond Tutu, of Capetown, when he spoke in Cardiff City Hall on 4 June 2000. 'There is no future without forgiveness, which will help heal the scars of the past,' he told an invited audience of 700. 'We have a tremendous capacity for evil, but the most important thing is that we have an extraordinary capacity for good.' The Archbishop thanked the people of Cardiff for campaigning against apartheid. The prayers and direct action of many people, including those in Wales, had led to the changes in his homeland of South Africa, he said.

The man who has kept a Cardiff village clean for twenty-six years swept up the Mall in a taxi on 28 November 2000, to collect an MBE, which was awarded to him in the Queen's Birthday honours list in June. Brian Richards, who was sixty-four years old and who had been sweeping the streets in Whitchurch since 1974, had a kind word and a smile for everyone he met as he wheeled his trolley and brushes around Old Church Road and Merthyr Road, Whitchurch.

Brian, an active member of Bethel Baptist Church, Whitchurch, was born in Pontypridd, and moved to Whitchurch with his parents when he was 1 year old. He worked at the Melin Griffith Tin Works, Powell Duffryn Engineering works and a private engineering company before joining the former South Glamorgan County as a member of the road-repair gang. He was a road sweeper in Radyr for ten years before transferring to Whitchurch.

This was the year that the Cardiff Bay Development Corporation wound up and was replaced by the Cardiff Harbour Authority; a water bus service between Cardiff and Penarth was inaugurated on the barrage lake and the *Spirit of Cardiff* set up a new powerboat record for navigation of the British Isles. The Tenovus Research Centre was opened by the Queen, accompanied by the Duke of Edinburgh and work began on the Cardiff Community Centre on the site of the former St David's Hospital, which was once the city's workhouse. The statue of the 2nd Marquess of Bute was moved from St Mary Street to the part of Bute Street that was later renamed Callaghan Square. What would the Butes have thought about the pop group Steps in concert at Cardiff Castle?

2001

Cup Finals at Millennium Stadium

History was made in May 2001 when the FA Cup final between Liverpool and Arsenal was played at the Millennium Stadium in Cardiff. The prestige event, watched on television by an estimated 80 million soccer fans throughout the world, was staged in Cardiff after the traditional venue, Wembley Stadium, London, was closed for redevelopment. At Cardiff, Liverpool came from behind to beat Arsenal 2–1 and the sound of the Liverpool anthem, 'You'll Never Walk Alone', rang out in the stands that usually echoed with the hymns and arias of rugby fans.

Undeterred by defeat, Arsenal returned to Cardiff in 2002 and won the FA Cup by beating Chelsea 2–0 and retained the coveted title in 2003 beating Southampton 1–0. In 2004, Manchester United lifted the cup at Cardiff by beating Millwall 3–0 and in 2005 Arsenal were victorious again, beating Manchester United 5–4 on penalties for the first time in FA Cup final history.

The redevelopment of Wembley stadium is scheduled for completion in 2006, and the London arena will again host the FA cup finals that brought joy and glamour to Cardiff at the beginning of the twenty-first century.

The generosity of the people of Cardiff and South Wales was rarely greater than in the late 1990s when they dug deep in their pockets to raise more than £2m to help build the Ty Hafan Hospice for terminally ill children. The building was erected in the grounds of Sully Hospital with money raised after the *South Wales Echo* launched an appeal, and officially opened by Prince Charles in 2001.

It was a former policeman and Royal Protection Squad officer, Dominic Jenkins, who spearheaded the drive to build the first hospice of its kind in Wales. As a Special Branch officer Dominic had acted as a bodyguard to members of the royal family, including the late Diana, Princess of Wales, who accepted his invitation to be the first royal patron of Ty Hafan. His dream was to build a ten-bed hospice to provide respite care for up to 300 terminally ill children and their families every year. He believed there had to be *cwtches*, to use the Welsh word for 'corners', where parents could just sit down and be quiet. There was a need for gardens and a play area, not just for the sick children but for their healthy brothers and sisters. Dominic saw his work partly as a thank-you to God for having three healthy children and four healthy grandchildren of his own.

The fund was boosted by millionaire philanthrophist Sir Julian Hodge. From time to time he offered to match money donated pound for pound, up to as much as a quarter of a million pounds. The Ty Hafan Hospice was just one of countless charities with which Sir Julian was still actively involved until his death in Jersey at the age of 99 in 2004. The first time he made a pound-for-pound offer to support a worthy cause was in 1978, when the *South Wales Echo* launched an appeal for £100,000 to build a modern orphanage in the grounds of Nazareth House, Cardiff. The *Echo* readers responded magnificently and raised £75,000 in just over twelve months, as a tribute to the excellent work carried out by the Poor Sisters of Nazareth since they opened a refuge for needy children in Newtown, Cardiff, in 1872. Sir Julian added a cheque for £25,000 to the total and was present when the completed house was officially opened by James Callaghan, the Cardiff MP who was Prime Minister at the time.

It was inevitable there would be a Cardiff link with the World Trade Center attack in New York on 11 September 2001, an attack that killed more than 3,000 people. Steve Evans, who had worked as a reporter at BBC Wales in Llandaff, was in one of the buildings when it was hit by a hijacked aircraft, and reported live from the scene. He was a BBC reporter in New York and was on camera when one of the towers collapsed behind him. He carried on broadcasting. Steve, who came from Bridgend, was close to the scene when a second plane crashed into the second tower. A third plane targeted the Pentagon in Washington, and a fourth attack was foiled by passengers when a hijacked plane crashed into a field in Pennsylvania.

Journalists with links to Cardiff have reported on major events throughout the world. Former *South Wales Echo* reporter Michael Buerk revealed the extent of the famine in Ethiopia, which led to Band Aid in the 1980s. Jeremy Bowen has reported on wars and major incidents. His father, Gareth Bowen, was editor of Radio Wales, and Jeremy's mother was a freelance photographer. Two boys from Splott were at the White House Press Conference at the time of the Watergate Scandal: John Humphreys, later linked with the *Today* programme on Radio Four, represented the BBC, and former *Echo* reporter Norman Rees was there for ITV. This was all in the tradition of Wynford Vaughan Thomas, a BBC war correspondent who flew in a Lancaster and reported on a 1,000-bomber raid on Berlin. Wynford was a doyen of HTV television until his death in 1987.

2002

Peace Gesture

Apart from the Pope's visit to Cardiff in 1982, the most important visitor to the city from Rome was Nigerian-born Cardinal Francis Arinze, the Vatican's expert on Islam and other major faiths. His visit, in the spring of 2002, came at a time when the world was still reeling from the hijacking of airliners used by terrorists to destroy the twin towers in New York City.

Relationships between Christians and Muslims were at an all-time low. The Cardinal's call in Cardiff to universities to promote an objective study of the growing religious and cultural diversity in the world and to encourage harmony and mutual understanding between cultures, was one of the greatest and most important statements to be made by a leader of the Catholic Church.

The Cardinal added that the courses he proposed should not be intended to preach or as an effort to persuade students to embrace one religion or the other but to make them aware of what other people believe, what rites they carry out and what code of conduct guides their lives. Cardinal Arinze said that every university should ask itself what provision it has made to enable its students to become informed of the major religions in their region, and indeed in the world. Even if a student in Britain wants to be an engineer, for example, he or she should not be ignorant of what Christianity, Judaism, Islam, Buddhism, Sikhism, Hinduism and the traditional religions believe, worship and do. Visiting scholars and religious leaders can help to whip up interest.

Cardinal Francis Arinze was presented with a miner's lamp during his visit to Cardiff.

2003

Iraq Injury

Cardiff-born Stuart Hughes, a BBC producer, was severely injured by a landmine while filming in Iraq following the 2003 invasion after returning to Cardiff, Stuart, whose parents lived in Rhiwbina, had part of a leg amputated. His cameraman was killed in the explosion. Stuart was one of the first journalists to report the surprise early handover of Iraqi sovereignty, filing his report to the BBC and blogging it on his own web site, for which he rightly claimed a world exclusive. He had obtained the story by lobbying a NATO conference in Turkey where he was working as a world affairs producer for the BBC, after joining BBC Wales in Cardiff.

It was in 2003 that the go-ahead was given for a memorial to mark the site of Cardiff's Little Ireland, the historic Newtown area of the city. The warren of streets with their tied-together houses had been demolished as part of a slum-clearance programme in the mid-1960s and the families rehoused in new estates at Trowbridge and Pentrebane. But the spirit of Newtown lived on in the hearts and minds of those whose ancestors had come to Cardiff around the time of the Great Irish Famine of the 1840s. They came with little more than the rags they were wearing, their Irish language and their Catholic faith, which flourished in the parish of St Paul's. Mary Sullivan (née Rafferty), who chaired the Newtown Association, was inspired to establish a memorial to the area by a poem written by Tommy Walsh, which told the story of Newtown and regretted that there was no plaque on the wall to mark the site. By 2005 there was more than a plaque – there is a monument on land in Tyndall Street depicting the layout of the streets in Newtown and listing the names of the families who lived there. The memorial was unveiled by singer Charlotte Church, whose grandparents had lived in Newtown. After the unveiling ceremony mass was celebrated at the Coal Exchange in Cardiff Bay – a complete contrast to the humble St Paul's Church which had served Newtown from 1873 to 1962.

In 2003 the National Historic Ships Committee recognised the importance of the *Waverley*, the last seagoing paddle steamer in the world. The boat, a frequent visitor to South Wales ports, was placed on the list of Designated Vessels. The *Waverley* was built in 1947 to replace one of the same name that had been built in 1899, had seen service in the First World War and which was sunk returning from Dunkirk in 1940. The *Waverley* was in good company on the list of historic ships, for among the seven vessels listed at the same meeting was the Royal Yacht *Britannia*.

2004

Tsunami Terror

Death and destruction came to eleven countries in Christmas week 2004, when an earthquake in the depths of the Indian Ocean caused tsunami tidal waves that killed 150,00 people and destroyed whole villages and towns. More than 25,000 people died in Sri Lanka and a million people were made homeless. Among those who escaped the disaster was Jennifer Hill who was on honeymoon with her husband Tony, a museum assistant at the Welsh Museum of Life at St Fagans and a former engineer at the Cardiff Royal Infirmary. They were staying at Club Palm Bay, Marawila, Sri Lanka, when the tsunami tidal wave destroyed the beach only yards from their holiday bungalow. Fortunately the wave was not as severe on their side of the island but it still swept away everything in its path.

On 5 January 2005, the First Minister at the National Assembly led three minutes' silence in Cardiff, in memory of more than 150,000 victims of the tsunami tidal waves. He was joined by Chancellor of the Exchequer Gordon Brown, who was in Cardiff to visit Gabalfa Primary School to talk to parents about the government's plan to endow newborn babies with gifts of money. The Chancellor was full of praise for the people of Wales who, within two weeks, had raised more than five million pounds to help the countries hit by the tsunami.

The Wales Millennium Centre in Cardiff, was officially opened over the weekend of 26/28 November 2004. It was the first national cultural institution to be built in Wales for over half a century and the UK's final lottery-funded Millennium Project.

The core facility of the £106.2-million centre is the main lyric auditorium, the Donald Gordon Theatre, named after the South African whose foundation donated £10 million to the project. Seating 1,900, the auditorium is designed to world-class acoustic and sight-line specifications for opera and for amplified sound. The technical and architectural quality of the principal performance space has been acknowledged by visiting companies as being matched only by the Royal Opera House. The building also contains a 250-seat studio theatre, dance studio, recording studio, orchestral rehearsal hall, shops, cafés and restaurants and a suite of small function and event rooms. The centre is also home to a range of resident arts companies, including the Welsh National Opera, Urdd Gobaith Cymru (Wales' leading youth organisation) and Diversions Dance Company (the national dance company of Wales).

The opening of Wales Millennium Centre was marked by a programme of celebration commencing with an opening ceremony on the afternoon of 26 November and running through to the Royal Gala evening of Sunday 28 November, when the Queen, the Duke of Edinburgh and Prince Charles were in the audience. The key to unlock the door of the Millennium Centre had already travelled around the world before arriving by boat in Cardiff, where it was passed through the hands of a human chain of around 500 people. The last person in the chain was Janet Thickpenny, a mother of two celebrating her fortieth birthday and she officially opened the WMC. The opening night concert was held with 1,000 tickets being won by ballot.

On Saturday evening an open-air family concert took place in the Roald Dahl Plass, with Owen Arwel Hughes conducting the Cory band playing pieces including 'Singing in the Rain' and 'You'll Never Walk Alone'. The finale was a spectacular fireworks display. A host of stars took part in the Sunday-night concert, including Charlotte Church, Bryn Terfel and Shirley Bassey, who was born about half a mile away from the centre, one of the finest in the world.

Phase 2 of the Wales Millennium Centre project, completing the outline of the city block and containing a rehearsal hall for the BBC National Orchestra of Wales, commenced in the spring of 2005.

Cardiff has produced many outstanding athletes, but none greater than Tanni Grey-Thompson, who was created a Dame in 2004 after winning eleven Olympic gold medals in paralympic events. Wheelchair-user Tanni has competed and won at world-class events ranging from 100 metres to the marathon. She has won six gold medals in the London Marathon.

Tanni was born with spina bifida in Cardiff in 1969 but her parents encouraged her to be independent. From St Cyres Comprehensive School, Penarth, she went to Loughborough University where she obtained an honours degree in Politics. Tanni has become BBC Wales Sports Personality of the Year three times and also named Welsh Woman of the Year. She was awarded the OBE in the year 2000.

Tanni is assistant head of the Potential Programme, which is developing the young disabled athletes who will form the nucleus of a squad for the Beijing Paralympics in 2008, a games in which Tanni is not expected to compete. She has also played a major role in helping Britain successfully bid to stage the 2012 Olympic and Paralympic Games. Tanni lives in Redcar with her husband, Dr Ian Thompson and their daughter, Carys, who was born in February 2002, but her heart is still very much with her native Cardiff.

2005

Death of Pope John Paul II

When Pope John Paul II died in Rome on 1 April 2005, the news was broken to BBC viewers and listeners by Cardiff-born Jeremy Bowen. Presenting the BBC news from Rome at the time was presenter Hugh Edwards, who had trained as a broadcaster at Radio Cymru in Llandaff, Cardiff. It was appropriate that two men linked to Cardiff should be involved in the biggest story for decades, relating to the Pope who was made a Freeman of Cardiff when he visited the city on 2 June 1982. As Jeremy Bowen told the world on the day of the Pontiff's funeral: 'There has never been a day like this, nor a Pope like this.' Hugh Edwards gave the main commentary for the funeral, at which Cardiff and Wales were represented by Archbishop Peter Smith.

When Pope Benedict XVI was elected on 19 April 2005, Hugh Edwards presented the special BBC news bulletin, and the religious expert who assisted him was another former BBC Wales journalist, Christopher Morgan, of the *Sunday Times*. Christopher was a member of St Luke's Anglican Church in Cowbridge Road East.

Former Prime Minister James Callaghan died in 26 March 2005, eleven days after his wife, Audrey. Lord Callaghan was first elected an MP for Cardiff in 1945 and held the offices of Foreign Secretary, Home Secretary, Chancellor of the Exchequer and Prime Minister in Labour governments. He was a Freeman of Cardiff. In April 2005, another Welsh political giant, Gwynfor Evans, died at the age of 92. He was President of Plaid Cymru for more than thirty years and the first Welsh Nationalist MP to be elected to the House of Commons when he won a by-election in Carmarthen in 1966.

Cardiff showed the world it was a capital of kind-heartedness and 'can-do' dynamism on 24 January 2005. Three weeks previously, Paul Sergeant, the General Manager of the Millennium Stadium, watched the terrible scenes of the tsunami disaster unfolding on his television and, like millions of people across the planet, felt he just had to do something. He thought big – let 60,000 people gather in the Millennium Stadium for a concert and raise £1 million.

Sergeant and his rainbow-striped jumper became a fixture on the news bulletins. He and his team began with a blank sheet of paper and a deadline that would frighten even the hardiest adrenalin addict. Concerts of this scale take six months to arrange – they had twenty-one days. On a drizzly Saturday, the home of Welsh rugby was transformed into a rock stadium. Thousands milled around a concrete pitch and giant stage erected on the try line. The closed roof shut out the grey afternoon as the stands filled with an audience as eclectic as the line-up of performers. Although Welsh flags and inflatable daffodils were dotted through the crowd, tickets had been sold as far afield as Aberdeen and Penzance. 'I pray the concert is a huge success,' Prince Charles declared from the video screens. And it was. At the end of those rainbow stripes, Sergeant had found gold – £1,248,963 to be exact.

Many tears were shed during the Holocaust Memorial Service which was held at Cardiff City Hall on 27 January 2005. It was an emotional occasion for the hundreds of people present, especially for the older people, who were no strangers to the genocide that killed more than six million innocent people, mainly Jews, but also Gypsies, non-Whites, political prisoners, Jehovah Witnesses, homosexuals, and anyone else who annoyed the hated Nazis.

But of all those present at the City Hall, none was more moved or affected than Edith Salter, an 84-year-old widow from Cyncoed, who arrived in Cardiff in 1946. For she survived the notorious Auschwitz consecration camp where more than a million fellow Jews were murdered by the Nazis; she saw her mother, father, grandmother and sister's one-year-old baby taken to the gas chambers in the Auschwitz killing factory in Poland. Edith, whose family name was Links, and her sister Rose, survived because they were fit enough to work.

Some months before the Russians liberated Auschwitz on 27 January 1945 Edith was one of fifty women who were taken to Germany and forced to work, making bombs in an underground factory. She was later taken to Hamburg, where she was eventually liberated by the British. After spending some time in Sweden, where she worked as a designer, she came to Cardiff in 1946 and studied at the College of Art for three years. In 1949 she married Frederick Salter, a lecturer in psychology in Cardiff. Their daughter and grandchildren live in London, Edith's sister Rose lives in Melbourne, Australia.

When Cardiff remembered the victims of the Holocaust in 2005, Edith joined the Lord Mayor, Jacqui Gascon, in lighting the memorial candle. It was the most poignant moment in what Edith described as a dignified and moving service. She added that it was good that her family and other victims are remembered and that the story of Auschwitz is made known to young people in the hope that what happened then will never happen again.

In 1905, the year that Cardiff was made a city, Wales beat the All Blacks at the Arms Park. In 2005, as Cardiff celebrated its 100th anniversary as a city, the Welsh rugby team made its own contribution to the occasion – by beating world champions England in Cardiff for the first time in twelve years and going on to beat Italy, France, Scotland and Ireland to win the Grand Slam for the first time in twenty-seven years. The cheers of the Welsh fans in the 70,000 crowd at the Millennium Stadium on 5 February echoed throughout the country when Gavin Henson landed the 42-metre winning penalty to beat England three minutes from time.

There was futher joy four days later when the Welsh soccer team beat Hungary 2–0 at the Millennium Stadium, with Celtic's Craig Bellamy scoring twice. The result was a triumph for one of Cardiff's greatest sporting heroes, John Toshack, for the match was the first of his second term as manager of the Welsh team in which he had starred as a player before managing Swansea City and teams in Spain. Tosh was also one of the great Liverpool team of the 1970s. Unfortunately Wales failed to qualify for the World Cup.

John Toshack's name has appeared on many programmes but it was something of a surprise to see it on the one published to mark the 150th anniversary of St John the Evangelist Church in Canton. The footballer's message read: 'My family has had close connections to the church and I have warm memories of attending the church as a youngster.' There was also a message from Derek 'Blue' Weaver, a member of the pop group Amen Corner/Strawbs. He remembered singing in the choir at St John's and paid a special thank-you to the choir leader for his teaching and patience.

The first service held at the church was in 1855. It was the first Anglican church built in Canton, and 150 years later it was still a central part of the community. The anniversary celebrations started in January with a concert by the Canton Café Orchestra. Throughout the year local schools and organisations joined in the festivities.

Billy O'Neill was almost as old as the City of Cardiff. He was born on 4 October 1907, twenty-three months after Cardiff was made a city but sadly he died at the age of 97 on 1 February 2005, as he was looking forward to joining in the 100th anniversary celebrations. It is a safe bet that he is standing outside the Pearly Gates with a collecting box in his hands, for Billy was one of the greatest supporters and collectors for charity that Cardiff has ever known. For more than thirty years he collected at local supermarkets and stood outside Cardiff Market on Saturdays collecting for Age Concern. The fact that he was drawing his own old-age pension did not bother him, as anyone in the Plasnewydd Friday Afternoon Friendship Club will tell you. Billy was secretary of the club for three decades and was still in office attending meetings up to December 2004, when he was taken ill.